HARRY STYLES

A SIGN OF THE TIMES

HARRY STYLES

A SIGN OF THE TIMES

ANNIE ZALESKI

G:

Page 2: Harry Styles at the 2021 Grammy Awards, March 14, in Los Angeles, California

G:

First published in the UK in 2024 by Gemini Adult Books Ltd, part of Gemini Books Group

Based in Woodbridge and London

Marine House, Tide Mill Way, Woodbridge, Suffolk, IP12 1AP

www.geminibooks.com

A CIP catalogue record for this book is available from the British Library.

ISBN 978-1786751577
Bound and printed in China

10 9 8 7 6 5 4 3 2 1

Book design: Adelle Mahoney
Editor: Jo Rippon

FSC
www.fsc.org
MIX
Paper | Supporting responsible forestry
FSC® C008047

CONTENTS

INTRODUCTION

On the surface, Harry Styles's path to stardom looks a lot like that of another teen idol: *NSYNC's Justin Timberlake. Both men catapulted to global fame with their former bands—and became fan favorites in the process—and both also launched solo careers on their own terms. In the early to mid 2000s, Timberlake created cutting-edge pop/R&B collaborations with futuristic beatmakers like Timbaland and the Neptunes; Styles, meanwhile, chose to draw from timeless retro sounds, including 1970s folk, soul and rock, as well as 1980s pop.

Dig a little deeper, however, and Harry's artistic ascent has parallels to the musical careers of several other legends. His willingness to take sonic risks and stay true to his muse echoes the attitudes of George Michael; the latter also left a successful pop group (the 1980s duo Wham!) for the freedom of being an iconoclastic pop star who cherished artistic integrity. Styles's approach to music also calls to mind Beatles icon Paul McCartney. Not only is Macca an adventurous solo artist—look no further than synthesizer experiments such as "Temporary Secretary"—but after the Beatles went their own ways, McCartney reinvented himself as the leader of another band, Wings; the latter gesture is reminiscent of how Styles himself now performs live with a core group of stellar musicians. And, in a more contemporary vein, perhaps there's also a little Madonna and Lady Gaga in the way Styles has branched out beyond music into fashion and movies.

Left: Harry Styles live onstage, 2022

But then again, it's also quite unfair to compare Styles to *anybody*, as he's a singular artist who has carved out his own unique path in the world. His solo albums reshape the boundaries of pop music, challenging listeners to think about mainstream modern music in a new way. "Harry inspires a feeling of, 'Let's do something we haven't done before,'" his long-time collaborator Kid Harpoon told *Music Week*. "He wants to make interesting stuff."

Styles's approach to fashion eschews strict gender binaries; he's appeared on the cover of *Vogue* wearing a dress and sported colorful, tattoo-baring jumpsuits as stage wear while on tour. He has also never been afraid to try new things, such as hopping in and taking the role as a fill-in host on a late-night network TV talk show at the last minute. And Harry Styles empowers fans to embrace their true selves in genuine, earnest ways—among other things, a favorite bit of concert banter is "Please feel free to be whoever it is that you want to be in this room tonight"—which has made his shows supportive, inclusive community gathering places.

An affable child, Styles grew up playing soccer and cheering on Manchester United. He showed an aptitude for words at an early age, and he said in the 2011 book *Dare to Dream: Life as One Direction*: "I could produce really good pieces of writing and I felt really proud when I got an A for my first ever essay." Life had other plans for him at the time, he added: "But I was so easily distracted that I started spending more and more time chatting to friends in class or daydreaming, and sadly I never quite got up to that standard again."

Of course, Harry rekindled this love of words years later via songwriting—but before that, there was music. Elvis Presley's tender 1960 hit "The Girl of My Best Friend" was "probably the first song I learned the words to," Styles said in a 2022 interview with Narduwar. "I used to sing it in my bedroom when I was a kid." Naturally, this was the first song he recorded when his grandfather gave him a karaoke machine as an eighth birthday present. In addition to Elvis, Styles listened to classic rock and nineties pop—and made quite an impression on the adults around him.

"I always knew he'd succeed at whatever he did because he'd always charm people," Styles's dad, Des, told *The Daily Record* in 2012. "From performing in the car or on holiday, he'd always be able to hold a crowd or hold a room, even when he was a kid." Sadly, Harry's parents divorced when he was seven years old, although his mom, Anne Twist, remained an especially supportive figure. In fact, she actually filled out Styles's

"I always knew he'd succeed at whatever he did because he'd always charm people... he'd always be able to hold a crowd or hold a room, even when he was a kid." DES STYLES

Above: Harry Styles shows support onstage for the LGBTQ+ community

Opposite: Performing live onstage at the 2023 Grammy Awards, in Los Angeles, California

application to audition for popular TV show *The X Factor*—which turned out to be a life-changing move, as his appearance on the show led to the formation of One Direction.

During the first half of the 2010s, the group absolutely dominated the global music landscape. Not only did the members of One Direction boast effervescent personalities, but their music also stood out from the crowd; in fact, they released a steady string of albums brimming with joyful pop tunes like "What Makes You Beautiful" and "Best Song Ever."

To the chagrin of fans, however, in 2016 One Direction took a career break. For many musical artists, taking this kind of action reflects a falling-out or acrimonious schism. However, nothing could be further from the truth with One Direction. Later on, it emerged that Styles had first broached the idea of a break in late 2014, because he valued One Direction's loyal supporters—"I didn't want to exhaust our fan base," he told *Rolling Stone*—and he also wanted to preserve the group's integrity. In fact, Styles just might be the biggest One Direction champion out there.

"When you leave a band or boy-band, you feel like you have to go the complete other direction and kind of say, 'Don't worry everyone! I hated it! It wasn't me!'" he said in the documentary *Harry Styles: Behind the Album*, which was released in conjunction with his 2017 self-titled debut album. "I loved it. I wouldn't be here if it wasn't for that band. And I don't feel like I have to apologize for that."

Indeed, Harry Styles has navigated the evolution rise from boy-band phenomenon to solo star rather seamlessly. Part of that is due to his grounded upbringing, which has kept him level-headed. "He's just the same as he has always been," his mom Anne Twist told *The Daily Mail* in April 2023. "As a very little boy, he was very much like he is now, just a smaller version." Styles's music reflects this self-assurance. "He's very

authentic to himself," Twist continued. "He takes his influences from what he feels, what he's listened to, what he likes. He's not thinking, 'Right, I need to make this song for this particular demographic.' He does what feels right to him—and it seems to be universally appreciated."

This intuitive way of making music has led to solo albums that *feel* modern—and fit right in on Top 40 radio—but don't necessarily conform to dominant contemporary trends. Styles's debut album took heavy influence from 1970s rock and pop; his follow-up, 2019's *Fine Line*, was inspired partly by the innovative genre-shapeshifter Joni Mitchell. And 2022's *Harry's House* touched on funk, soft rock, and R&B, amongst other genres.

Outside of music, Styles has remained true to himself and his moral compass, advocating for things like gun control, Black Lives Matter, and LGBTQ+ rights. And his support for the queer community predates his solo career: During a 2014 One Direction tour stop in St. Louis, Missouri, Styles wore the jersey for Michael Sam, the first openly gay player drafted into the National Football League.

Unsurprisingly, Styles has had a marked influence on the music world as a whole. Both Milky Chance and Jorja Smith have covered his 2022 hit "As It Was," while the eighties icon Rick Astley—another pop star who knows a little something about success at a young age—also covered the tune on New Year's Eve 2023. Where Harry Styles will go next in his life *and* career is anyone's guess. But you can be sure that whatever it is will be interesting, unexpected *and* colorful.

Right: Harry Styles poses with his awards backstage at the 2023 BRIT Awards

"As a very little boy, he was very much like he is now, just a smaller version. He's very authentic to himself." ANNE TWIST

CHAPTER 1:

STORY OF MY LIFE

Harry Styles is standing at a microphone, sporting shaggy hair and a dapper suit, ready for one of the biggest performances of his life. As his band kicks into Bryan Adams's "Summer Of '69," he looks down intently, clearly concentrating on making sure his vocals are on point. The focus pays off: When Styles starts singing, he sounds self-assured, nailing every note of the rocker with hints of vibrato and an abundance of passion.

At first, a couple of women near the front of the stage are distracted—talking to each other, fixing their hair, and looking for their friends. By the second verse, however, Styles and the band have won them over, and they've started gleefully dancing and pogoing. Even Styles hitting a few rough notes—understandably, since "Summer Of '69" does have some difficult high-register moments—can't stop the good vibes.

Incredibly enough, this footage wasn't from a One Direction gig or a solo concert—but of sixteen-year-old Harry Styles singing lead for his scrappy rock band White Eskimo at the wedding of a friend's mom. The performance was a rather last-minute gig. Styles later recalled the group ended up having to learn twenty-five songs (including Bob Marley tunes requested by the bride) in a matter of days. The quartet was paid £160 (British pounds)—equivalent to a little less than $200 (US dollars)—split equally between the four of them.

At the time, White Eskimo was earning some local notoriety; among other things, they won the 2009 Battle of the Bands at Styles's place of learning, Holmes Chapel Comprehensive School. They were also dabbling in writing original tunes, including one called "Gone In A Week" that Styles could still quote verbatim years later. "It was

Previous Page: Harry Styles holds a photograph of himself as a young boy as he greets fans during a visit to Holmes Chapel, in the UK

Opposite: Harry Styles at 3 years old

"I've always liked being around people and getting to know new people." HARRY STYLES

about luggage," he told *Rolling Stone*. "'I'll be gone in a week or two/Trying to find myself someplace new/I don't need any jackets or shoes/The only luggage I need is you.'"

This stint with White Eskimo gave Styles a small taste of music success, enough to make him crave more time in the spotlight. However, his early upbringing didn't necessarily point to him becoming a global superstar.

Harry Styles was born on February 1, 1994, in Worcestershire, England, the second child of Anne Twist and Desmond "Des" Styles. (Older sister Gemma had arrived first, four years before.) By all accounts, he was an outgoing, polite kid who had a lot of friends and got along well with others.

"I've always liked being around people and getting to know new people," he said in the 2011 book *Dare to Dream: Life As One Direction*. Accordingly, he added that his "earliest memories" involved being at Disney World as a five-year-old—and having an absolute blast. "Everything seemed so big and fun and I loved it."

Growing up in Holmes Chapel—a village in Cheshire, England, where his family had moved to set up home—Styles soaked up all different kinds of music. His mom gravitated toward more modern pop artists such as the eighties-inspired Savage Garden, jazz-influenced Norah Jones, and country icon Shania Twain. In contrast, his dad, who worked as a financial advisor, loved Elvis Presley, as well as classic rock bands such as the Rolling Stones, Queen, Pink Floyd, and Fleetwood Mac. The latter group loomed particularly large in his world.

"In my family we listened at home, we listened in the car, we listened wherever we could," Styles said in his 2019 speech inducting Fleetwood Mac's Stevie Nicks into the Rock and Roll Hall of Fame. "'Dreams' was the first song I knew all the words to, before I really knew what all the words meant. I thought it was a song about the weather. But I knew it was a beautiful song about the weather."

It's clear in hindsight to see how these formative listening experiences inspired Harry and influenced the music he would later create. But early on, both parents recognized their son's potential. "I used to listen to a lot of the music [my dad] was playing," Styles told *Rolling Stone*. "He'd play Elvis Presley to death, the Stones. I'd sing along to that and he'd say, 'You're going to be famous,' or whatever." His mom, meanwhile, once corrected Simon Cowell after *The X Factor* judge claimed that mothers might have a skewed perspective on whether their kids have talent. "He said, 'Mums don't always know,'" she told the *Daily Mail*. "But I always thought [Harry] had something."

Above: Des Styles, Harry's Dad, pictured in 2014

Opposite: "Dreams" by Fleetwood Mac. The first song Harry learned to sing.

Indeed, this wasn't a case of parental bias. At age five, Styles made his stage debut at Hermitage Primary School in Holmes Chapel, portraying a church-dwelling mouse named Barney. "I had to wear my sister's tights," he told *Rolling Stone*, "and a headband with ears on it, and I had to sing a song all by myself." An adorable video of this performance captures Styles's preternatural charisma. It's not terribly obvious that the tiny child onstage is a future superstar, but his reactions and hand gestures are crisp and on beat—no small feat for such an acting novice.

In the coming years, young Styles would experience some big life changes, starting with his parents divorcing when he was seven years old. "I remember crying about it when my parents told me they were splitting up, but after that I was alright," he said in *Dare to Dream*. "I guess I didn't really get what was going on properly, I was just sad that my parents wouldn't be together any more." Although the breakup's aftermath was as positive as it could be ("Feeling supported and loved by my parents never changed," he said years later) Styles was particularly close to his mom; in fact, post-divorce, he and Gemma went to live with her when she moved out of Holmes Chapel. "Since I've been 10, it's kind of felt like—protect mom at all costs," he told *Rolling Stone* in 2017. "My mom is very strong. She has the greatest heart."

Styles was nine years old when his mom remarried, to a man named John Cox. The couple ran a pub in Cheshire called the Antrobus Arms, with the family living above the premises. "I remember the first night, it was like a night where a band was playing, and I just thought, 'How am I going to get to sleep?'" Styles told *Rolling Stone*, referencing the noise emanating from the pub. However, he added that he eventually became used to hearing the music—and even learned some guitar basics from a rocker who "used to be in Deep Purple or something" that occasionally played at the pub.

Years later, Cox reminisced that Styles unsurprisingly loved the Antrobus Arms's convivial atmosphere, and would frequently hang out with the adults. "He was the centre of attention," he told the *Daily Mirror*. "He was really lively and would run around the pub, with all the customers fussing over him." Cox also fondly remembers singing Frank Sinatra's "(Theme From) New York, New York" with a young Styles at

"'Dreams' was the first song I knew all the words to, before I really knew what all the words meant. I thought it was a song about the weather. But I knew it was a beautiful song about the weather."

HARRY STYLES

"Since I've been 10, it's kind of felt like—protect mom at all costs. My mom is very strong. She has the greatest heart." HARRY STYLES

another pub's karaoke night. "He is a down to earth kid and always has been."

When he was a teenager, Styles would experience yet another big life change. Cox and his mom split up, which led to a move back to Holmes Chapel. Not long after, Harry's mom met and started dating a man named Robin Twist. This time, it was her turn to be protective of her kids; Styles recalled in *Dare to Dream* that she was cautious about having Robin coming over to their house. "She worried about it a lot, so in the end I used to text him and tell him to come over because I thought he was a really cool guy."

Overall, however, Harry's adolescence was rather unremarkable, distinguished by the usual things teenagers go through as they navigate growing up. Despite his affable demeanor, he told *Rolling Stone* he "had a phase of listening to really heavy music. Not stupid heavy, but a bit ... just because I thought it was cool." His clothing rebellion was charmingly tame: It took the form of wearing black clothes and Nirvana T-shirts.

Like many teens, he also had a job in order to pick up some extra spending money. Styles spent Saturday mornings behind the counter at W Mandeville Bakery, helping customers while sporting a white collared shirt and a striped maroon apron. "I started at five and finished at four in the afternoon, and got like 30 quid," he told *Rolling Stone*. "It was a joke."

Styles noted after he no longer worked there, he did miss the baked goods he'd receive on his break. But he was still working at the bakery—and singing with White Eskimo—when he tried out for *The X Factor* in April 2010. "Winning the battle of the bands and playing to that many people really showed me that's what I wanted to do," he said in an interview for the show. "I got such a thrill when I was in front of people singing. It made me want to do more and more."

Harry seemed to audition for *The X Factor* as if it was a lark. "I remember looking at the young guys on there—and I was kind of like, 'I'd love to have a go at it just to see what happens,' and that was kind of it," he later recalled to *Rolling Stone*, noting that his mom actually filled out his application. At the time of his tryout, he was equally blasé when telling the judges why he decided to audition, casually saying, "I've always wanted to audition but I've always been too young, so I thought I'd give it a whirl this time."

During his interview in front of the judges and a studio audience, he looks adorable (and adorably nervous) talking about himself. However, he drew laughs when judge Simon Cowell asked him what sweets were in demand at the bakery. "The Viennese fancy is always a favorite," he said. "The millionaire's shortbread." At the time, he

"I'd gone because my mom told me I was good from singing in the car ... but your mom tells you things to make you feel good, so you take it with a pinch of salt." HARRY STYLES

had just finished his GCSEs (General Certificate of Secondary Education) and was planning on studying law, sociology and business in college.

For his audition, Styles chose to sing Train's "Hey, Soul Sister." Although he looks quite earnest and at one point flashes a dimples-heavy smile at the audience, his vocal delivery is sadly wavering and off-key. Cowell recognized that the music might have been affecting his concentration and asked him to sing something *a cappella*. Styles chose Stevie Wonder's "Isn't She Lovely"—and sounded markedly more self-assured.

Harry then faced a critique from Cowell and the other judges. "For 16 years old, you have a beautiful voice," Nicole Scherzinger told him. Louis Walsh was less enthusiastic, saying, "I agree with Nicole. However, I think you're so young, I don't think you have enough experience or confidence yet." Speaking in his usually direct way, Cowell sided with Scherzinger, observing, "I think with a bit of vocal coaching, you actually could be very good."

In the end, although Walsh voted not to let him move forward on the show—a decision that drew a loud chorus of boos from the crowd—the other two judges voted yes. Years later, Styles reminisced about what it felt like to run through this gauntlet. "In that instant, you're in the whirlwind," he told *Rolling Stone*. "You don't really know what's happening; you're just a kid on the show. You don't even know you're good at anything. I'd gone because my mom told me I was good from singing in the car ... but your mom tells you things to make you feel good, so you take it with a pinch of salt. I didn't really know what I was expecting when I went on there."

To be fair, nobody expected that Styles's time on *The X Factor* would become what it did—or possess a roller-coaster's worth of unexpected twists and turns. But appearing on the show also ended up changing his life—and kickstarted a career that continues to go beyond even his wildest dreams.

CHAPTER 2:

THIS
IS US

Redemption stories don't get much better than the origins of One Direction. The five members of the group—Harry Styles, Liam Payne, Louis Tomlinson, Niall Horan, and Zayn Malik—originally auditioned for the seventh season of *The X Factor* as soloists. Unfortunately, all five were on the brink of elimination, with Styles's shaky take on Oasis's "Stop Crying Your Heart Out" putting his status in jeopardy.

However, fate intervened. During the bootcamp portion of the season, three of the show's judges (Simon Cowell, Nicole Scherzinger and Louis Walsh) decided to put together a boy band from the existing pool of contestants. The trio pored over Polaroids of these aspiring vocalists, intent on assembling a group that possessed that elusive "X factor."

Footage from this strategy session is illuminating: Scherzinger especially saw potential in the future members of One Direction, gushing first over the fact that Horan, Tomlinson and Styles looked good together. "They're just too talented to get rid of," she added. "And they've got just the right look and the right charisma onstage. I think they'll be really great in a boy band

Previous Page: December 7, 2010. One Direction visit the home of Harry Styles, Holmes Chapel, Cheshire, UK.

Right: One Direction (L–R): Liam Payne, Louis Tomlinson, Harry Styles, Zayn Malik, and Niall Horan

together." Comparing them to "little stars," she observed, "You can't get rid of little stars—so you put them all together."

The judges settled on a boy band after adding Payne and Malik into the mix—and on July 23, 2010, One Direction was officially born. "This is a lifeline," Cowell told the excited crew when they found out about their second chance. "You have got to work 10, 12, 14 hours a day, every single day, and take this opportunity. You've got a real shot here, guys."

As we all know now, that ended up being a vast understatement. Although One Direction inexplicably ended up finishing third on *The X Factor*—solo artists Matt Cardle and Rebecca Ferguson landed in first and second place, respectively—they went on to sell millions of records and become one of the biggest, most beloved pop bands in the world. Reaching this status didn't come easy, of course: Cowell was correct in saying that achieving this kind of success requires hard work and dedication. And over the next few months, One Direction spent every possible moment refining their craft and figuring out how to be a successful band.

It all started during the judges' house round in Marbella, Spain, where the newly minted group worked up two *a cappella* songs: Natalie Imbruglia's "Torn" and Kelly Clarkson's "My Life Would Suck Without You." Styles took a prominent role in both choruses, belting out the lovelorn, anguished hook of "Torn" and embracing his pop star side on Clarkson's tune. Cowell was satisfied enough with the performances to send One Direction into the next round. All of the boys were emotional, but Styles especially was overwhelmed (in a good way) with happy tears in light of the decision.

One Direction's meteoric rise to fame started once *The X Factor*'s live episodes kicked off in October 2010; in fact, adoring screams wafted from the audience throughout the first episode, during which the group performed an uptempo, almost Broadway-esque version of Coldplay's "Viva La Vida." Unfortunately, Styles's nerves reared their ugly head the week after and he felt ill, though he rallied as One Direction reprised their cover of "My Life Would Suck Without You." The upbeat version impressed Cowell, who said: "You are the most exciting pop band in the country today."

By the third week, which found the group indulging their power ballad side with a soaring take on P!nk's "Nobody Knows," One Direction hysteria was starting to take off. "It's like five Justin Biebers!" judge Walsh exclaimed after the performance, as the cheering crowd nearly drowned him out as he spoke. Footage of the band going shopping resembled a small-scale Beatlemania, as they were greeted by flashing cameras

Opposite: Harry Styles and Louis Tomlinson, 2010

"... when he went off to *The X Factor* house I said to him, 'Keep true to who you are, Harry, don't turn into an arse. You'll still have to unload the dishwasher when you get home.'" ANNE TWIST

Previous Page: Harry Styles performs during *The X Factor* live show, November 27, 2010

Left: One Direction arrive for an autograph signing session at HMV in Bradford, UK

and ecstatic fans; one excited teenage girl exclaimed repeatedly, "He winked at me!" Styles's penchant for pranks had also become tabloid fodder. "My favorite party trick is to wear nothing but a gold thong in the house," he told the *Daily Mirror*. "My friend bought it for me for my birthday." Another *X Factor* group, Belle Amie "say I prance around the house in it," he added cheekily. "I'd say it's more of a slow, gentle stroll."

Harry's mom observed that such antics were very much in character. "I know I'm his mum, but he really is a lovely young man and he's coming across exactly as he is at home," Anne told *Now*. "But when he went off to *The X Factor* house I said to him, 'Keep true to who you are, Harry, don't turn into an arse. You'll still have to unload the dishwasher when you get home.'" Indeed, Styles's soft-hearted side emerged when he went home for a visit during the season and had a tender moment with his mom. "No matter how big and famous you become, you'll always be my baby," she said, with tears in her eyes, just before embracing him. "I love you very much."

On October 30, One Direction tackled a cover of Bonnie Tyler's "Total Eclipse Of The Heart" for *X Factor*'s Halloween-themed week. In a fitting nod to the song's origins—composer Jim Steinman wrote it as a love song for vampires—the group sported red eye make-up and fake gashes on their necks. The group easily moved into the Top Ten, with judge Dannii Minogue saying, "You are a boy band doing exactly what a boy band should do ... I want to come to your party."

During the next few weeks, One Direction indulged their pop-rock side with an anthemic cover of Kim Wilde's new wave classic "Kids In America"—which sounded tailor-made for the group—and showed off their burgeoning vocal maturity with a cover of Elton John's majestic anthem "Something About The Way You Look Tonight." The crowd response ramped up considerably when Styles launched into a solo; he responded with a poised performance. Cowell was also impressed by what he heard, saying, "This is the first time in all my time in *X Factor* that I genuinely believe a group will win *X Factor.*"

Week after week, viewers tuned in as the group's self-assurance and chemistry grew—and One Direction continued to amass more and more fans. The group excelled when tackling rock songs, particularly a brisker, R&B-leaning arrangement of the Beatles' "All You Need Is Love." And Styles had a particularly good week when the group performed two classic tunes: the Joe Cocker-popularized "You Are So Beautiful To Me" and Bryan Adams's "Summer Of '69." The former suited Harry's range and demeanor, and as he poured his heart into the gorgeous song, the camera zoomed in for a close-up shot of his face. The golden-brown lighting and his tousled haircut made him resemble a 1970s teen heartthrob.

After the group's spirited version of "Summer of '69," Cowell went out of his way to point out that Styles, who was wearing a Rolling Stones T-shirt, picked the song—a fitting but unsurprising choice, since he knew the tune quite well from his days fronting White Eskimo. However, the song pick also illustrated his quiet confidence as a leader: Not only did Styles know his strengths as a vocalist—he was already working to amplify the strengths of One Direction.

At this point, however, tensions were high, as the group had made it to the Top Five of the show. But One Direction leapt into the finals with ease thanks to a fantastic production of Rihanna's "Only Girl (In The World)" and a note-perfect version of Snow Patrol's aching "Chasing Cars." During the two-day finals event, they continued to steamroll forward with a take on Elton John's "Your Song"—another tune perfectly suited to Styles—and a duet with fellow (one-time) boy band member Robbie Williams.

As *The X Factor* wound down, One Direction did an in-store signing at an HMV record shop in Zayn Malik's hometown of Bradford, and an outdoor live gig in Wolverhampton. Both events drew hundreds of supportive fans, who braved cold December weather to scream, cheer and yell for the group; it was clear that momentum was on One Direction's side going into the finals. But, as mentioned previously, in a shocking turn of events, the group came in third for the season, eliminated after performing Natalie Imbruglia's "Torn" on the second night of the finals. The quintet

Below: One Direction at the Heart
FM studios in London, 2011

Overleaf (L-R): Harry Styles,
Louis Tomlinson, Liam Payne,
Zayn Malik, and Niall Horan of
One Direction pictured with their
award for Best British Single, at
the 2012 BRIT Awards

> # "You are a boy band doing exactly what a boy band should do... I want to come to your party." DANNII MINOGUE

looked absolutely devastated, but gamely and politely congratulated the eventual runner-up, Rebecca Ferguson, and did a brief live chat after hearing the bad news.

Despite the setback, optimism shone through from their judge and mentor, Simon Cowell. "This is just the beginning for these boys," he said. Once again, this would prove to be a massive understatement. By late January 2011, One Direction had signed a huge record deal with Cowell's label, Syco, and were in the US laying the groundwork for a debut album with the producer RedOne, who had previously found major success with Lady Gaga. Not long after, the group took a break to release a book (*One Direction: Forever Young: Our Official X Factor Story*) and perform on The X Factor Live Tour, and then resumed work on their own music. In the midst of this incredible whirlwind of activity, Styles celebrated his seventeenth birthday.

As with many high-profile pop albums, One Direction's debut was a globe-spanning production. The group recorded in Los Angeles, London and Stockholm, Sweden, and cut songs co-written by stars such as Ed Sheeran and Kelly Clarkson, as well as A-list songwriters Steve Robson (Rascal Flatts, Take That) and Toby Gad (Beyoncé, Fergie, Demi Lovato). *The X Factor's* vocal coach, Savan Kotecha—who had also written hits for Usher and Britney Spears—co-wrote One Direction's official debut single, "What Makes You Beautiful." (A lovely cover of Alphaville's "Forever Young" was slated to be One Direction's debut single had they won *X Factor*; alas, it wasn't meant to be.)

Lyrical inspiration came to Kotecha when he was in London with his wife. "She was having a bad morning," he told *The Hollywood Reporter*. "She was like, 'Oh, I feel so ugly' and I was like, 'No, you look beautiful. You don't know how beautiful you look.' And I was like, 'Oh, crap! That's a good song! Hold on!'" Styles loved the song, Kotecha added. "When he heard the demo, I was in Miami on my way back to Sweden, and he sent me a text message saying, 'I think you got it. I think you got the one here.'" In a subsequent MTV UK interview, Styles elaborated on what drew him to the song: "I think for us we wanted to release something that wasn't cheesy but it was fun. It kind of represented us, I think it took us a while to find it but I think we found the right song."

An airtight power-pop song that shows off the group's sparkling personalities and effervescent harmonies, "What Makes You Beautiful" was indeed the perfect introduction to One Direction. Released on September 11, 2011, after premiering on BBC Radio 1 the previous month, the single unsurprisingly went straight into the UK charts at No. 1 and eventually took home the 2012 Brit Award for British Single

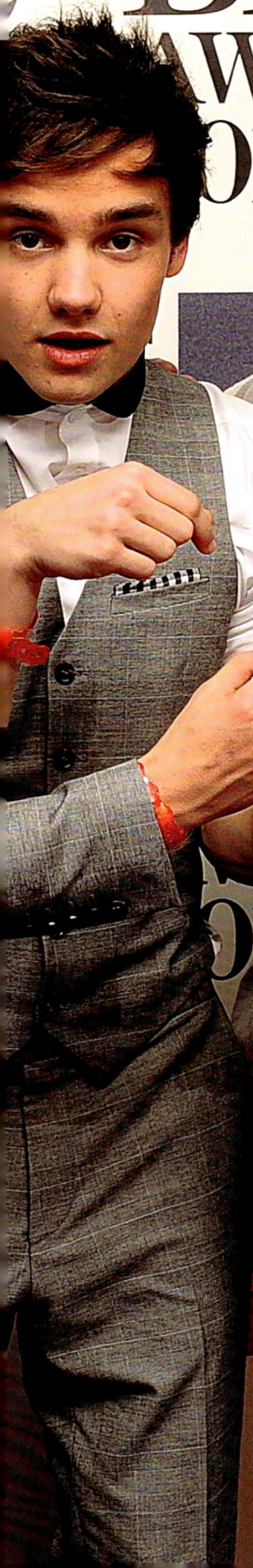

Opposite: Signing autographs for fans in New York City, 2012

of the Year. Over time, it sold millions of copies around the world and became One Direction's signature song.

Styles still plays "What Makes You Beautiful" in his solo shows. It's easy to see why: For starters, he takes lead vocals on the chorus, meaning he's the careful steward of the song's heartfelt expressions of love and desire. But "What Makes You Beautiful" also captured the inclusive, positive vibe and ethos espoused by One Direction—and, by extension, Styles. If anything, the song served as a blueprint for his entire career.

In November, One Direction signed an American record deal with Columbia Records; in the UK and other parts of the world, they also released their debut album, *Up All Night*. Although at heart a collection of pop songs, the full-length also nods to classic rock, seventies singer-songwriter fare, adult contemporary ballads, and the polished anthems favored by nineties boy bands. Styles had co-writing credits on several songs, including "Taken"—on which he also shows off his tender vocal side, despite lyrics chiding someone who is only attracted to unavailable people—the dance-pop trifle "Everything About You" and Keane-like "Same Mistakes."

Up All Night was a rousing success, debuting at No. 2 in the UK and spending seven weeks in the Top Ten. Upon its March 2012 release in the US—a date mere weeks after Styles celebrated his eighteenth birthday—the album was an even bigger

"… we wanted to release something that wasn't cheesy but it was fun. It kind of represented us, I think it took us a while to find it but I think we found the right song." HARRY STYLES

smash. It topped the *Billboard* 200 albums chart, making One Direction the first UK group to debut at No. 1 with their first album. "What Makes You Beautiful" was also a success stateside. Bolstered by remixes by Dave Audé and Lenny B, the single reached No. 1 on *Billboard*'s Dance Club Songs chart and peaked at No. 4 on Hot 100 singles chart.

When One Direction started doing promotion in the US, the response was as overwhelming (and positive) as it was in the UK. The day before *Up All Night*'s release, nearly fifteen thousand fans converged on New York City's Rockefeller Plaza bright and early in the morning for the group's national TV debut. One Direction made an appropriately grand entrance, traveling to the stage atop a double-decker bus emblazoned with their logo and then taking their places onstage in front of their dapper-looking band.

"New York City, make some noise!" Styles yelled, the cue for everyone to kick into "What Makes You Beautiful." Fans waved Union Jack flags and held up signs that said things like "Kiss Me"; when One Direction later left the main stage to sing on a tiny round stage, the crowd reached out their arms toward the group members, hoping for even the smallest touch. As it turns out, this feverish response was just a small taste of what was to come for One Direction in the future. Things were just getting started.

Right: One Direction perform on the Today *show in New York City, March 12, 2012*

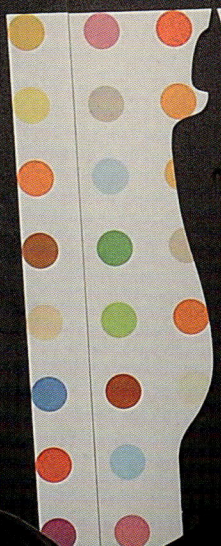

CHAPTER 3

BEST SONG EVER

By early spring 2012, One Direction was a bona fide phenomenon. In the UK, the group had charted five singles, including three that had reached the Top Ten, and embarked on the sold-out *Up All Night Tour*. In America, One Direction had opened shows for fellow boy band Big Time Rush and announced headlining tour dates to promote their No. 1 album *Up All Night*. Unsurprisingly, the US leg of the tour was a hot ticket: The band's show at the legendary arena Madison Square Garden sold out in less than ten minutes.

In June 2012, One Direction pulled off another astounding feat. Their concert film *Up All Night: The Live Tour* sold 76,000 copies during its first week of release in the US—outselling the best-selling music album that same week, John Mayer's *Born and Raised*, which sold 65,000 copies. Understandably, all of these milestones meant that some people started comparing One Direction to the Beatles. Speaking to VOA (Voice of America)'s Larry London that July, Styles modestly denied that parallel. "If you base your career on trying to achieve someone else's goals, it is the wrong way to do it. We like to achieve things ourselves. We kind of find it a bit ridiculous because the Beatles are such an icon."

Still, there was no denying that One Direction's career ascent came with the kind of attention similar to that of other teen idols like the Beatles. In interviews, Styles was asked questions about things like his hair regimen ("It's kind of like, out of bed and then dry it," he told one interviewee. "Put stuff in it. It usually stays up") and favorite color, while during the *Up All Night Tour*, One Direction incorporated a segment where they addressed Twitter (now known as X) queries. At the Houston show, one user asked the band members to do the shoulder thrust they did on *The X Factor*—Styles obliged the request with a cheeky smirk on his face—while another asked, "What's your favorite thing about Texas?" Harry's response drew massive cheers: "The accent."

Previous Page: One Direction with their Global Success Award at the 2013 BRIT Awards

Left: Backstage at BBC's Children in Need, November 16, 2012

Opposite: Harry Styles performs onstage with One Direction in front of fans at the Rockefeller Plaza, New York City, 2012

Watching footage of this tour is fascinating in hindsight. Styles received his fair share of delirious audience screams, but he didn't necessarily have more time in the musical spotlight than his bandmates. This illustrates how talented each member of One Direction is—and how, at this point, it wasn't necessarily obvious (or a given) that Styles would go solo.

On the downside, One Direction's increased popularity meant that every move Styles made came under the microscope. Naturally, this scrutiny especially applied to his dating life because he was linked to (or rumored to be linked to) multiple celebrities. In a fall 2012 interview with UK tabloid the *Daily Mirror*, he addressed claims that he was a womanizer ("I don't like going crazy-crazy, I like having fun but it's nice to wake up in your own bed, isn't it?") and downplayed the wildness of his dating status: "I'm an 18-year-old boy and I'm having fun. I'm just not having as much fun as people make out."

Among other things, Styles was likely to be referring to his 2011 relationship with future *Love Island UK* host Caroline Flack, which drew heavy tabloid coverage primarily because of their age gap; Flack being older. However, he was in the spotlight once again in late 2012 when he briefly dated Taylor Swift. The two notoriously shared a cozy date at the Central Park Zoo; were spotted hand-in-hand in England; and then kissed at midnight after she performed on *Dick Clark's New Year's Rockin' Eve with Ryan Seacrest*. By early 2013, however, things had cooled off between them after a vacation in the British Virgin Islands.

Time has softened any hurt feelings between the duo—in fact, they've been spotted catching up at the Grammy Awards in 2021 and 2023. And, years later, Styles was kind to his younger self when reminiscing about the Central Park date. "When I see photos from that day I think: Relationships are hard, at any age," he told *Rolling Stone*. "And adding in that you don't really understand exactly how it works when you're 18, trying to navigate all that stuff didn't make it easier. I mean, you're a little bit awkward to begin with. You're on a date with someone you really like. It should be that simple, right? It was a learning experience for sure. But at the heart of it—I just wanted it to be a normal date."

Still, none of these things detracted from the music or Styles's desire to make sure One Direction kept evolving. "It's good if you don't have a moment where you go, 'You know, I've made it,' because I think it's important that you keep changing up your goals

"I'm an 18-year-old boy and I'm having fun. I'm just not having as much fun as people make out." HARRY STYLES

and stuff to make sure you don't kind of take your foot off the pedal," he told a reporter. "I think you have to keep making sure that you're always on top of your game."

That growth came to light on One Direction's second album, *Take Me Home*. Released in November 2012, the record featured many of the same songwriters that appeared on *Up All Night*, including Styles. He co-wrote the brisk pop gem "Back For You"—a reassuring song where the narrator always comes back to their special someone—and the mellower, string-swept "Summer Love"; the latter is a meditative, melancholy look back at an ephemeral love affair. For good measure, Styles also had a hand in writing two bonus tracks: The harmony-heavy, heart-on-sleeve ballad "Irresistible" and the pop-punk-inspired plea for forgiveness "Still The One."

Preceded by the smash single "Live While We're Young," *Take Me Home* sold 540,000 copies in the US during its first week on sale—triple the number *Up All Night* sold in week one—and easily reached No. 1 on the *Billboard* album charts. In the UK, both the album and the single "Little Things" debuted at the top of their respective charts; One Direction were the youngest group ever to pull off this feat. Fittingly, they won Best International Artist at Australia's 2012 ARIA Awards—the first of five straight wins in this category.

The group closed out the year on the road—a trek that included TWO appearances in one week at Madison Square Garden. After their long-sold-out headlining concert (which featured an epic cover of Wheatus' 2000 hit "Teenage Dirtbag" and a surprise guest appearance from Ed Sheeran on a song he co-wrote, "Little Things") One Direction played a short set at the radio station-sponsored Z100 Jingle Ball just four days later. For the second year in a row, the quintet also acknowledged their roots and made a guest appearance on *The X Factor UK* live final.

As the calendar turned to 2013, things continued to go One Direction's way. The group booked a massive world tour that started in February and continued into early November. They released a Comic Relief benefit song that mashed together Blondie's "One Way Or Another" and the Undertones' "Teenage Kicks." Called "One Way or Another (Teenage Kicks)," the snappy, rock-oriented tune peaked at No. 1 in the UK and demonstrated the band's ever-expanding sound. At the 2013 American Music Awards, One Direction won Favorite Pop/Rock Album for *Take Me Home* and Pop/Rock Band/Duo/Group Award—and they also won the 2013 BRITs Global Success award, an award they would win again the following year.

Opposite: Taylor Swift and Harry Styles, December 2012

However, not everyone was exactly head over heels for One Direction. In February 2013, Styles won Best Villain at the annual *NME* Awards. The honor didn't seem to signify any suspect behavior on his part ("I don't really feel like I've done anything that bad," he said after the nomination) but did acknowledge that SOME people were jealous of his teen idol status. However, he clearly took the win in his stride. "And thank you to @NME for my award tonight," Styles tweeted in response. "Gotta take the rough with the smooth eh?"

One Direction also won Worst Band that year at the *NME* Awards, which was far more insulting: The dig wasn't grounded in reality but indicative of a backlash against their popularity—and the inherent lack of respect given to boy bands like One Direction, in no small part because their fanbase is predominantly teenage girls, a group whose tastes are often dismissed or not taken seriously. Fans understandably bombarded *NME* with hate mail, causing the publication to run a story excerpting some of the more notable messages under the headline, "These One Direction Fans Are Really Angry."

A note from a fan named Jasime summarized why snotty dismissals of the band stung so much: To supporters, One Direction represented MUCH MORE than just a musical group. "To me, they're the reason I smile," Jasime wrote. "They are the only hope I have when everything has fallen apart. Their message, lyrics and music pick me up out of my hopelessness."

Buoyed up by so much love, One Direction ignored the haters and made moves to elevate their artistry. In July 2013, they released a new single, the effervescent power-pop tune "Best Song Ever," which reached No. 2 on both the US and UK singles charts. The song came

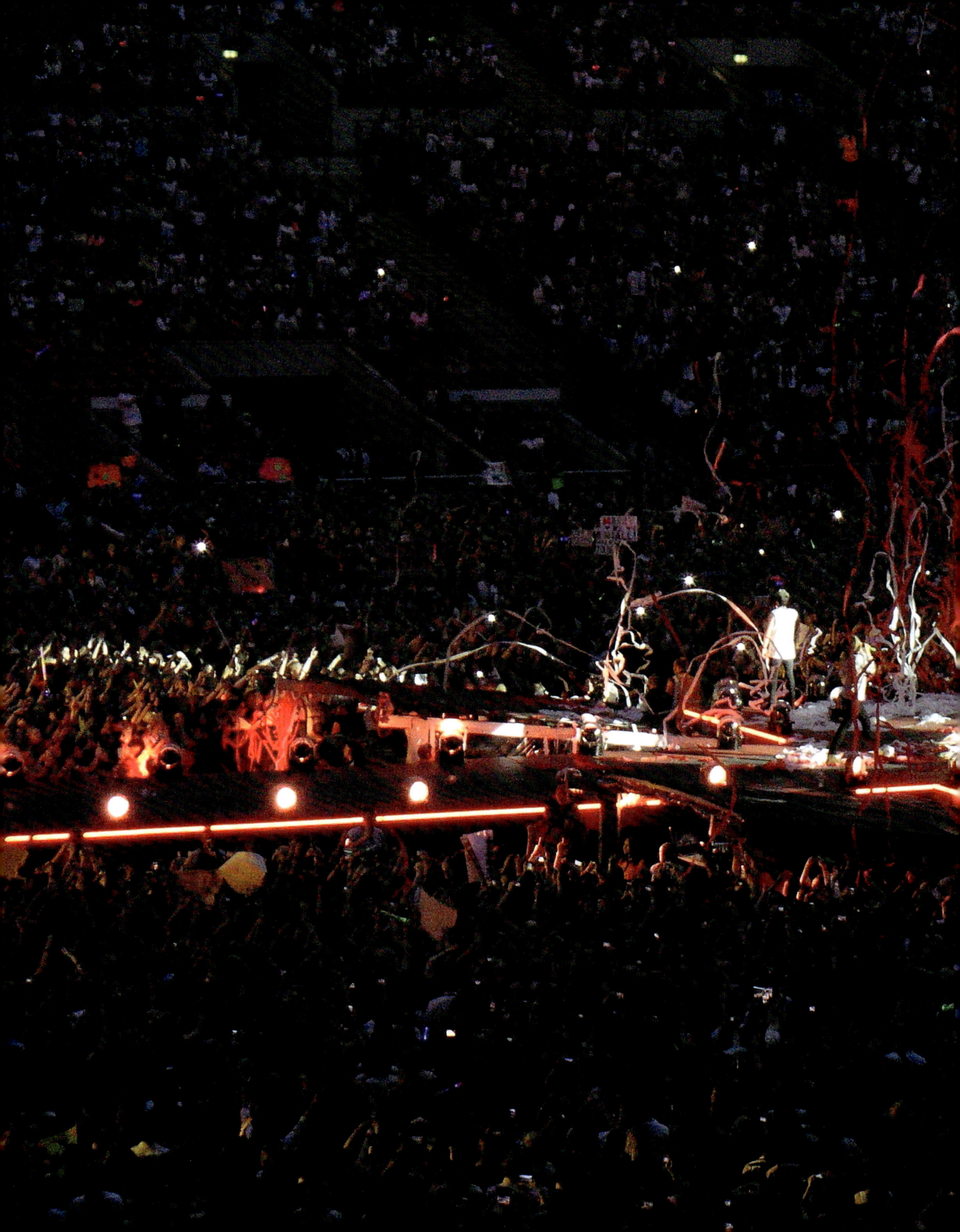

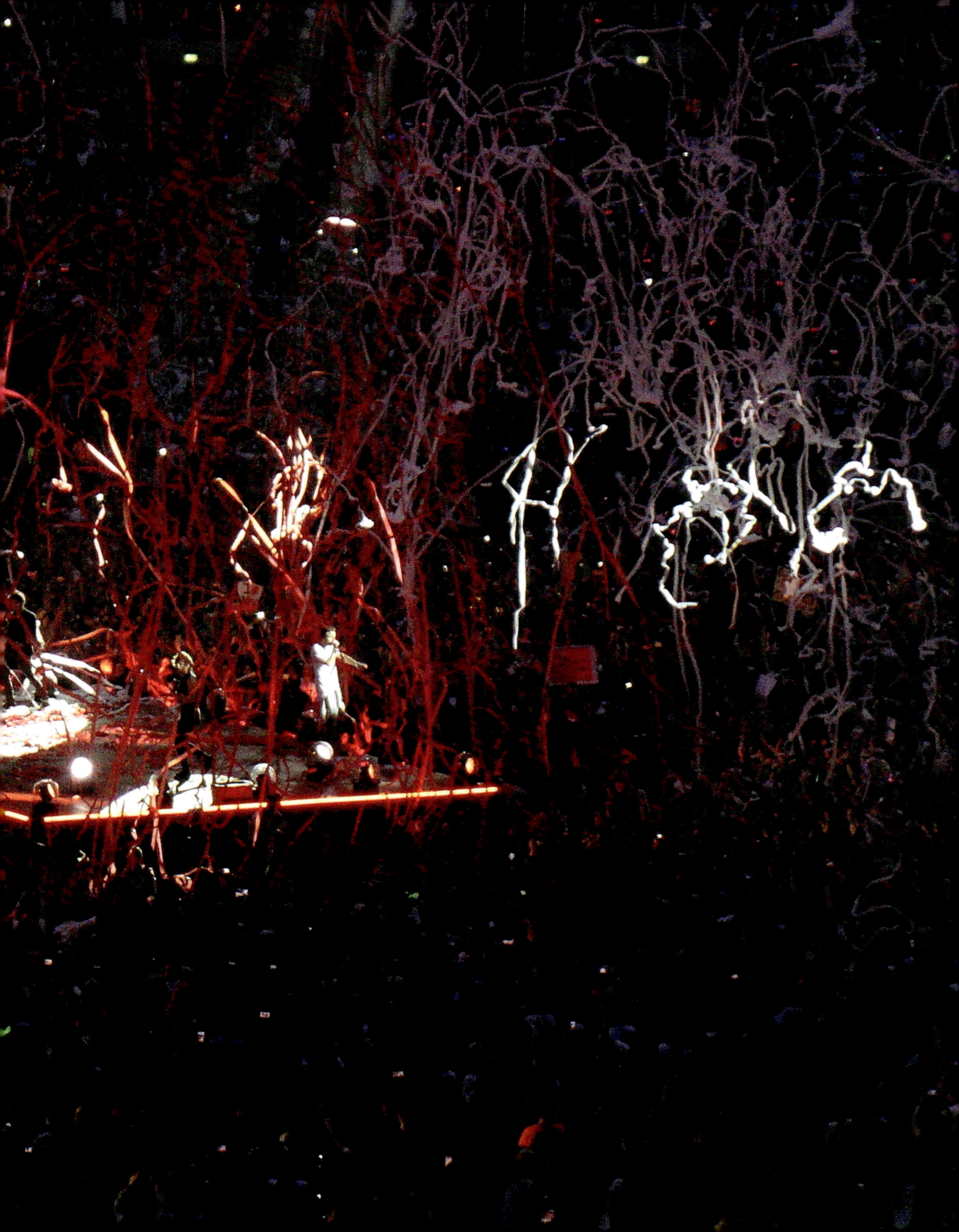

with a hilarious six-minute music video co-written by comedian James Corden. The clip mocks One Direction's burgeoning fame via a plot featuring out-of-touch industry executives—played by the band members themselves in disguise—attempting to sell the quintet on eye roll-worthy movie ideas and outfits.

Styles charmingly portrays a marketing guy named Marcel, envisioning the role as an earnest nerd who's trying (but failing) to impress his bosses and the group. In the end, the members of One Direction destroy the executive office and end up throwing a dance mob; the vibe is unmistakably (and favorably) reminiscent of the sly, humorous scenarios favored by the Monkees on their TV show. The "Best Song Ever" video set a record at the time for first-day views of 12.3 million.

The single appeared on 2013's *Midnight Memories*, which once again topped the charts around the world and broke sales records. In the UK, *Midnight Memories* sold 237,000 copies in a week—making it the fastest-selling album since a Michael Bublé Christmas album set charts ablaze in 2011—while in America, the full-length sold a whopping 546,000 copies.

Styles had slightly more co-writes this time around, highlighted by the lovelorn ballad "Story Of My Life," which reached No. 2 in the US and UK. However, the creative environment in which he wrote his *Midnight Memories* songs foreshadowed his solo career: He worked with small groups of songwriters that sometimes (and sometimes not) included additional members of One Direction. With OneRepublic ringleader Ryan Tedder, he wrote "Right Now," a sweeping pop song about pining for someone far away; alongside producer Jacknife Lee and Snow Patrol's Gary Lightbody, he wrote the earnest "Something Great."

The indie-folk tune "Happily"—in which a narrator pledges eternal fidelity as a way to coax someone to stay in a relationship—was even more important to Styles; in fact, it's not a stretch to say it was the pivotal point in his career. The song "was the first time I saw my name in the credits," he told *Rolling Stone* years later. "I liked that. But I knew I'd only sing part of it. I knew if I wrote a really personal song, I wouldn't sing it."

Styles described having other voices around him to handle these kinds of lyrics as "like a safety net," he added. "If a song was too personal, I could back away and say, 'Well, I don't have anything to do with it.' The writing was like, 'Well, if I was going to write a song about myself, I'd probably never sing it.'" But with the benefit of seeing things in perspective, Styles understood that as his songs evolved, he might change his

Previous Page: One Direction play Wembley, London, June 7, 2014

Opposite: Harry Styles arrives at the American Music Awards, 2014

"I don't think you can ever get used to being this famous. . . It's me right now in front of you and in the papers—but it's not all of me." HARRY STYLES

mind about performing such introspective material. "As the songs got more personal," he told *Rolling Stone*, "I think I just became more aware that at some point there might be a moment where I would want to sing it myself."

However, Harry wasn't quite ready for a solo career just yet. In 2014, One Direction booked their first stadium tour, the Where We Are Tour, which traveled to South America, Europe, the UK and North America. The time they had spent on the road made a big difference, as the group demonstrated the kind of confidence that suited the larger venues; Styles in particular sported a longer hairstyle and all-black outfits that exuded rock 'n' roll swagger. Among the highlights of the tour was a three-night, sold-out stand at Wembley Stadium, an honor dampened somewhat by the fact that Styles developed tonsillitis. "I was miserable," he told *Rolling Stone* years later. "I remember I came off, got in the car, and just started crying because I was so disappointed."

In between tour dates, One Direction found time to record and release another album, 2014's *Four*. Musically, the collection marked a turning point for One Direction, as the group had writing credits on the bulk of the record. Styles especially had more of a hand in the recording process, co-writing the pensive UK Top Ten hit "Night Changes"—which features a restless woman who feels lost but has a significant other offering grounding reassurance—and the equally stripped-down "Fools Gold," a song about falling for someone who's fake but irresistible. On the more upbeat side, Styles also co-wrote the galloping, mesmerized-by-romance tale "Stockholm Syndrome" and the shout-from-the-rooftops pop tune "Where Do Broken Hearts Go"; the latter features someone who's crushed the heart of a significant other and is trying (but not succeeding) at mending that fence.

Left: One Direction at the book signing for One Direction: Who We Are *in London, 2014*

That being said, *Four* isn't necessarily a massive sonic departure from *Midnight Memories*, although it did show the band's evolution. "We all liked the sound that we ended up with on the last one," Styles said in an interview. "We wanted an extension of that, while growing a bit. The thing is, we're all growing up at the same time, so it's good for us because the album's naturally progressed just as we do." *Four* once again reached No. 1 around the world, including in the UK and US; in fact, One Direction became the first group ever to have their first four studio records debut at the top of the charts.

Still, there were cracks in the successful facade. Zayn Malik left One Direction in March 2015, leaving the group to tour stadiums as a quartet on the forthcoming On the Road Again Tour. By this time, however, Styles was a seasoned enough performer to handle these bumps in the road, and he didn't necessarily feel too nervous performing live—although he admitted that it took a bit of time to get into the groove. "The fear of it has turned into adrenaline," he told *GQ* in 2015. "Definitely the first few shows you're scared as that's when all the mistakes happen. And then once you get your bearings and you know what you're doing you can enjoy it more."

Of course, even at the height of One Direction's popularity, Styles was quite unflappable and level-headed about fame—and firm about protecting his privacy. "I don't think you can ever get used to being this famous," he told *GQ*. "I've learned how to keep things separate or at a distance. I've nothing to hide. But seeing this as work, like a job, means I can take a step back. It's me right now in front of you and in the papers—but it's not all of me."

This attitude was rooted in self-preservation and personal experience, as One Direction's booming career meant the unassuming kid from Holmes Chapel was now a global superstar. But even as the group achieved milestones like stadium tours and multiple number-one albums, Styles was starting to think about his own future—and what was next.

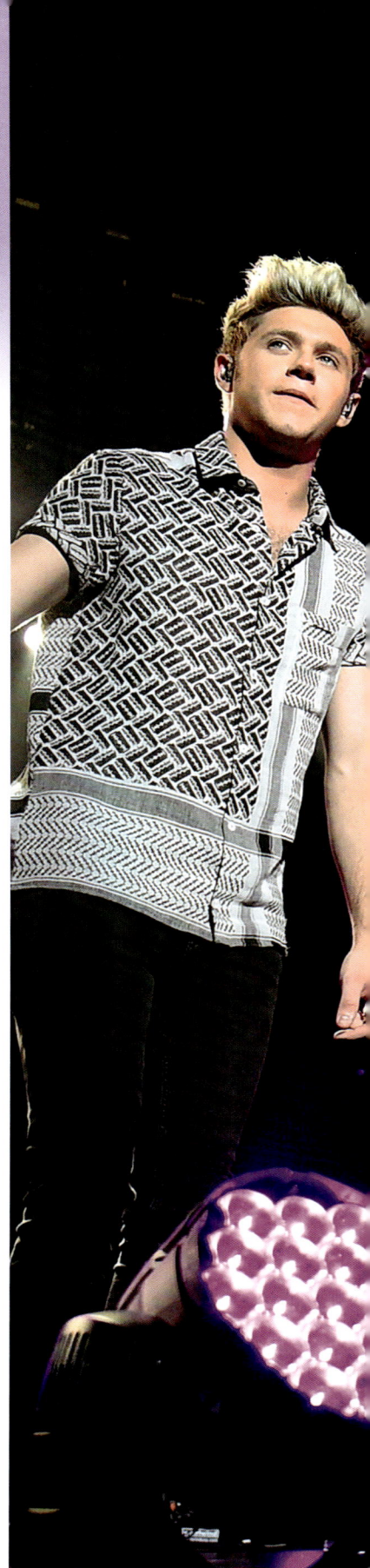

SONGWRITER

Harry Styles has long had aspirations to be a songwriter. In fact, he was writing songs for other artists while still in One Direction. Although tunes he co-wrote earmarked for Augustana ("Better Than Being Alone") and Gavin DeGraw ("Not Our Fault") have never actually surfaced—their existence was merely confirmed either via social media or through the songwriting database ASCAP, where Styles was sometimes listed as a writer under the name "Mick Greenberg"—other tunes have made a splash in the pop world. Here are five songs Styles co-wrote for other artists that did surface which made serious waves.

Ariana Grande, "Just a Little Bit of Your Heart" (2014)
Co-written with Johan Carlsson of the band Carolina Liar, "Just a Little Bit of Your Heart" appeared on Grande's second studio album, 2014's *My Everything*. The sparse, sighing piano ballad features lovelorn vocals and sweeping strings—a fitting backdrop for longing lyrics featuring a narrator who wishes they were the ONLY person a crush liked. Failing that, however, they'll take even a small part of their beloved's heart. Styles appeared to write "Just a Little Bit of Your Heart" on a whim. As Grande told MTV's *Total Ariana Live*, she was in the studio and he happened to be there. "And literally, [songwriters] Johan [Carlsson] and Savan [Kotecha] were like, 'Hey, do you want to write something for Ariana?'"

Opposite: Alex Kinsey and Sierra Deaton of Alex & Sierra, 2014

Left: Ariana Grande, 2014

Left: Jack Antonoff performs with his band The Bleachers, 2015

And he was like, 'Sure, mate.' And he just did." The song became a highlight of *My Everything*; Grande even performed the song during the 57th Annual Grammy Awards ceremony.

Alex & Sierra, "I Love You" (2014)

Styles also allegedly co-wrote "I Love You" with Johan Carlsson for Alex & Sierra (aka Alex Kinsey and Sierra Deaton), a musical duo who won the third season of *The X Factor US*. An emotional duet about a couple who still have feelings for one another despite being apart, the song is credited to the writer "Mick Greenberg" in the ASCAP database. However, fans did some sleuthing and figured out it appeared to be the case that Styles and Greenberg were one and the same. Alex & Sierra, who included the song on their 2014 debut album, *It's About Us*, seemed to confirm this guess in an interview with *Entertainment Tonight*. "We were told that Mick Greenberg wrote it," Kinsey said coyly. "That's what we were told, that's all we know. It could be Shaq! We don't know... Shaquille O'Neal might have written it." However, later in the interview the duo offered another tasty hint: "Maybe Mick and Taylor [Swift] are really good friends ... Maybe Mick & Taylor had a fling!"

Michael Bublé, "Someday" (2016)

Styles co-wrote "Someday," a bittersweet song about hoping that one day you'll reunite with a great love, with pop star Meghan Trainor and Johan Carlsson. A folksy, bittersweet duet between Trainor and Bublé, the song appeared on the latter's ninth studio album, 2016's *Nobody but Me*. Bublé caught wind of the song via Carlsson, when it was just a demo with Styles and

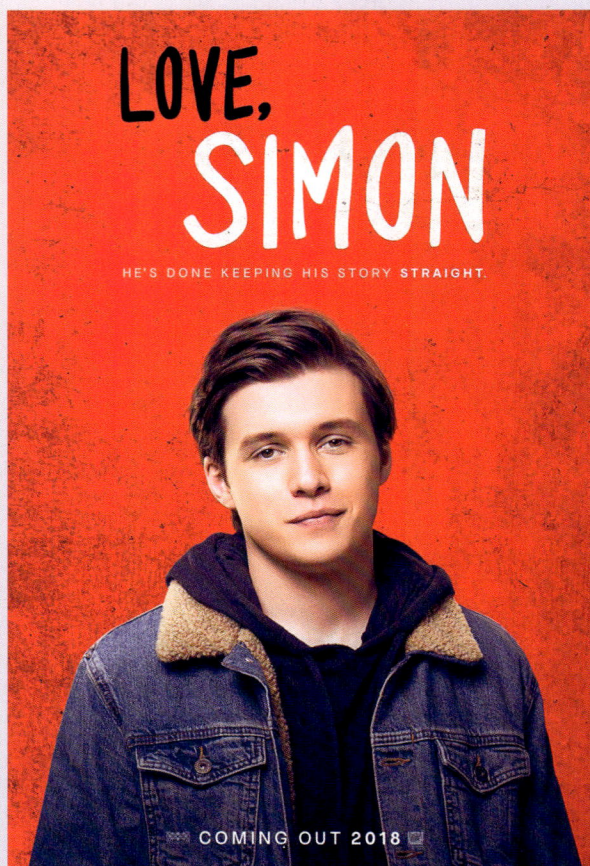

Left: Love, Simon *US movie poster, 2018*

Opposite: *Country singer Cam, 2020*

Trainor singing the song to ukulele accompaniment. "It was really beautiful," Bublé said, adding, "I've never recorded an original that I didn't write. But I loved it." Thanks to songs like "Someday," *Nobody but Me* ended up being nominated for a Grammy for Best Traditional Pop Vocal Album.

Bleachers, "Alfie's Song (Not So Typical Love Song)" (2018)

Bleachers—the synth-heavy eighties pop project helmed by Jack Antonoff—channeled the glory days of John Hughes teen movies with the saxophone-adorned "Alfie's Song (Not So Typical Love Song)." A nostalgic, poppy remembrance of the honeymoon period of a relationship when things were perfect, the tune appeared on the soundtrack for the 2018 rom-com *Love, Simon*. Antonoff told *Coup de Main* the song had initially come together during an earlier studio session with Styles and co-writer Ilsey Juber. "We were just messing

around with melodies and ideas," he said. "We didn't write that whole song, we just wrote parts that became that song. But [Harry's] just absolutely lovely, and a very good writer." When Antonoff started thinking about music for *Love, Simon*, "Alfie's Song (Not So Typical Love Song)" sprang to mind. "I went back and I was like, 'Oohhh, I want to change these lyrics and the verse and mess with this, make it my own.'"

Cam, "Changes" (2020)

The country artist Cam had previously crossed paths with Styles via an opening slot for him at Nashville's famed Ryman Auditorium. And as it so happens, she also worked with Tyler Johnson, who was also one of Styles's close collaborators. Through Johnson, Cam heard a demo of the folksy song "Changes" sung by the Americana star Lori McKenna that featured Styles on backing vocals and whistling. The tune—which was co-written by Styles, McKenna, Johnson and Kid

"I trust Harry's writing. I feel like he tries so hard to be himself in his music, and he doesn't take it lightly."

CAM

Harpoon—ended up making the cut on Cam's 2020 album *The Otherside*. It was unusual for her to include a song she didn't write, but Cam had nothing but praise for Harry's songwriting. "I trust Harry's writing," she told Apple Music. "I feel like he tries so hard to be himself in his music, and he doesn't take it lightly." The song's deep meaning also resonated, she added: "It was amazing to hear a song that someone else wrote that clicked so much with me personally. It's about feeling like you've outgrown where you're from, and you don't really want to admit that. It's kind of an uncomfortable thing to say, but I love when things are uncomfortable."

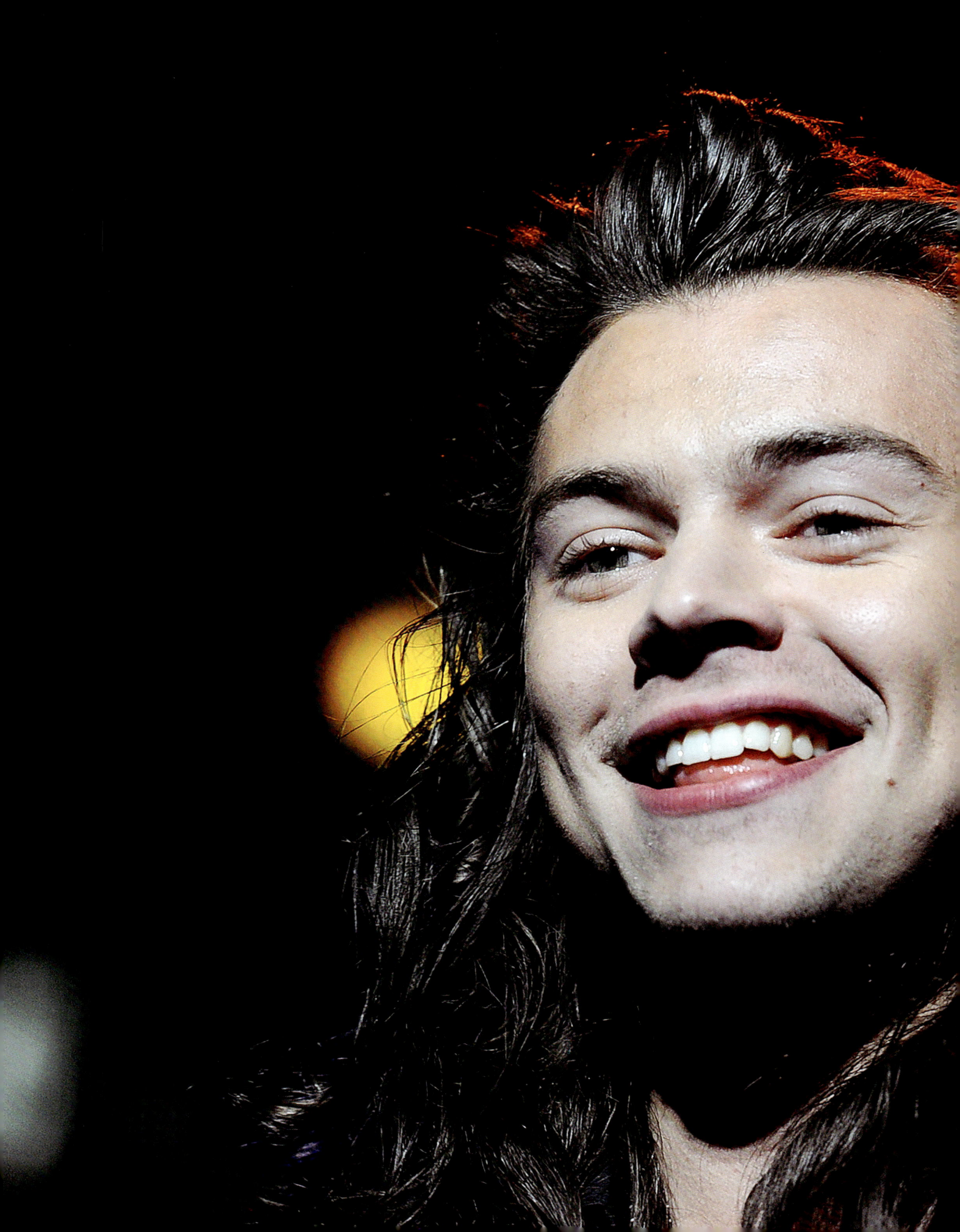

CHAPTER 4:

SIGN OF THE TIMES

"There was definitely a vibe of making [the album] the best it can possibly be, and knowing it has to last as long as it needs to." JULIAN BUNETTA

August 2015 brought some incredibly distressing news for One Direction fans: The group appeared to be on the verge of breaking up. Niall Horan took to social media to offer some reassuring words, clarifying that One Direction were taking a "well-earned break at some point next year," but it soon became clear that this break might be more permanent than people were letting on.

For starters, the band planned out this time-off in advance. In an interview with *Billboard*, songwriter-producer Julian Bunetta said that the possibility of a break loomed over the recording sessions for One Direction's forthcoming fifth studio album, *Made in the A.M.* "There was definitely a vibe of making [the album] the best it can possibly be," he said, "and knowing it has to last as long as it needs to until we make another record—if we make another record."

If that comment wasn't ominous enough, UK tabloids also started reporting rumors that Sony Records was angling to sign Styles to a solo record deal. Representatives issued swift denials—and, for the rest of 2015, One Direction embarked on what amounted to something between a victory lap and a long farewell. The group booked a summer US stadium tour, followed that up with more concerts in the UK and Ireland, and then made the rounds of high-profile radio festivals and TV shows. They also continued racking up honors, such as their second straight Artist of the Year win at the American Music Awards.

In November, One Direction released *Made in the A.M.* Like their other albums, it was a rousing global success, reaching No. 1 (or at least coming close to that

Previous Page: Harry Styles, 2015

Above: *Members of One Direction perform on Good Morning America, 2015*

Opposite: Harry Styles,
December 2015

peak) around the world. Styles also co-wrote several tracks on the album, that, in hindsight, foreshadowed the sonic directions he'd explore as a solo artist. These songs included the tender, string-swept piano ballad "If I Could Fly"—during which Styles showed off a smoky tone while taking a solo turn on the first verse and chorus—and "Olivia," a psychedelic-pop gem bolstered with a whimsical full orchestra recorded at Abbey Road Studios.

Songwriter Julian Bunetta told *Rolling Stone* that "Olivia" represented "Harry's genius," as the Beatles-esque song arrived in a burst of inspiration after a few days of writer's block. "At the very end of the day when Harry was going to leave, he was sort of saying the chorus phrase, so we just sat there and wrote it really quick," he said. " ... That was an incredibly adult, musically indulgent song that we all had a lot of fun making."

Styles's third co-write—the midtempo pop-rock ballad "Perfect"—was also quite sophisticated, although lyrically it's a rather mischievous ode to a no-strings-attached romance. Some suspected the song was about his short-lived relationship with Taylor Swift, although Harry demurred on specifics. "I think people interpret songs in different ways," he told *People*. "I'm never going to tell someone what a song's about because I feel like it's up to them." Adding to the mystery, Styles later claimed in a track-by-track interview that the song is "not that romantic" despite its references to late-night drives and secret trysts in hotel rooms. "It's not like a Romeo-Juliet type, 'I want to be with you forever, I wanna marry you, I wanna have kids with you,' [song]," he said. "It's more like, 'I'm not perfect, I really like you and if you wanna have fun this could be great' type thing."

"Perfect" ended up becoming One Direction's second-to-last chart hit, and one of the songs the group performed at their last live appearance to date: closing out 2015 on the annual TV special *Dick Clark's New Year's Rockin' Eve with Ryan Seacrest*. That same week, internet sleuths dug up more evidence of a burgeoning Styles solo career: four compositions in a song publishing database registered with him listed as the performer.

As the calendar turned to 2016 and the dust settled on One Direction's hiatus, whispers that Styles would be branching out on his own grew louder. A few months later, those long-gestating rumors came true: The musician signed a high-profile management deal in March and then, a few months later, formed his own independent record label, Erskine Records. That was followed by inking a solo deal with Columbia Records, the major label that had released One Direction's albums.

"Every decision I've made since I was 16 was made in a democracy. I felt like it was time to make a decision about the future... and maybe I shouldn't rely on others." HARRY STYLES

Speaking to *Rolling Stone*, Styles stressed how much he cherished One Direction—"I love the band, and would never rule out anything in the future. The band changed my life, gave me everything"—but was also clear about why it was so important for him to go solo. "I wanted to step up," he says. "There were songs I wanted to write and record, and not just have it be 'Here's a demo I wrote.'" Harry added that he wanted more say over his own destiny, too—and career direction. "Every decision I've made since I was 16 was made in a democracy. I felt like it was time to make a decision about the future ... and maybe I shouldn't rely on others."

To that end, Harry set up a business deal where he would technically license his music to Columbia via Erskine Records—thereby giving him more control and ownership over his solo records. And he also knew that he needed the right collaborators to make his vision a reality. Enter Jeff Bhasker, who had previously worked with rapper Kanye West, electro-funk maestro Mark Ronson, and the rock band Fun. All of these artists found pop success with striking original music, making Bhasker a perfect choice to be executive producer as Styles found his solo sound.

On the production side, Harry also assembled a crew of like-minded collaborators. In addition to Bhasker, he worked with producers Alex Salibian, Tyler Johnson and Kid Harpoon. Their backgrounds tended to include creative partnerships with artists who disliked being pigeonholed. Johnson received a Grammy nomination for his engineering work on Taylor Swift's *Red*—an album known for toeing the line between pop, rock, and country—and also co-wrote the folk-rock hit "Burning House" by the country artist Cam, while Salibian worked with iconoclastic solo acts such as Mikky Ekko and Elle King.

Kid Harpoon, meanwhile, had credits on Florence + the Machine's anthemic hits "Shake It Out" and "Never Let Me Go"—and had dabbled in writing with Styles before. "I just remember thinking, 'Man, when he does his album, I want to be there because this guy is special,'" he later told *Billboard*. As it turned out, Kid Harpoon ended up co-producing and co-writing two songs on *Harry Styles* (Styles's debut), "Carolina" and "Sweet Creature," but would have an even bigger influence on subsequent albums.

Bhasker and his team also used their connections to help Styles put together a band for the recording sessions, another crucial step in the creative process. Among the

Opposite: Harry Styles at LAX International Airport, Los Angeles, 2016

musicians they recruited was a jazz-loving guitarist and drummer named Mitch Rowland, who quickly became a trusted writing partner *and* touring band member. "He was working in a pizza shop and had never been in a studio," Styles said in the documentary *Harry Styles: Behind the Album*. "It felt like we kind of had each other to work out together and that helped it have someone who had no preconceived notions about me or who I was or anything."

With this new crew in place, Styles didn't rush his creativity *or* inspiration. He took his time putting the album together, traveling to familiar places such as England and California as well as new locales. In the fall of 2016, Styles spent two months working on music in Jamaica at Geejam, a secluded studio near Port Antonio. "It felt like a little secret," he said in *Behind the Album*. "It's fun to feel like no one knows where you are. It made such a difference from being in a busy city. It created this, like, total 360[-degree] writing experience that I've never had before."

These focused, extended sessions were a luxury, especially compared to the compressed timelines under which One Direction worked. And the lack of a public microscope was a boon for his creativity: Styles and his collaborators wrote six songs that ended up on the album a short time after arriving. "Jamaica was the happiest time I've had in a while," he said in *Behind the Album*. "It just felt like there was no pressure, at all."

The pressure-free environment helped Styles open up and write about his own life experiences. For example, certain songs reportedly drew on his alleged one-time romantic dalliance with model and reality star Kendall Jenner. Rumors that the pair were dating began when

Harry was still in One Direction, and crested around the start of 2016, when the couple were spotted hanging out together on yachts. Years later, even Jenner was curious about Styles's creative inspirations. "I'm dying to know this: Which songs on your last album were about me?" she asked him in December 2019, when the pair appeared together on *The Late Late Show with James Corden* and played the truth-or-dare-like game, "Fill Your Guts or Spill Your Guts." Styles was so against revealing specifics, he chose to take the dare and eat cod sperm instead.

For Harry, being so deliberate and thoughtful about his solo debut was important. He was trying to figure out what he wanted to sound like—and, musically, who he wanted to be—outside of One Direction. Being true to himself while finding his solo voice was also absolutely crucial. "I think it was tough to really delve in and find out who you are as a writer when you're just kind of dipping your toe each time," he told *Rolling Stone*, referencing his One Direction days. "We didn't get the six months to see what kind of shit you can work with. To have time to live with a song, see what you love as a fan, chip at it, hone it and go for that ... it's heaven."

Technically, Styles wasn't the first member of One Direction to go solo and find his niche. That honor went to Zayn Malik, who departed the group in 2015 and enjoyed chart-topping success the following year with both a single ("Pillowtalk") and an album (*Mind of Mine*). Malik dug deep into contemporary pop and R&B, which suited his voice perfectly and made the transition to a solo career much easier. Styles, however, was determined to follow his muse—even if it pulled him in against-the-grain directions that weren't necessarily contemporary.

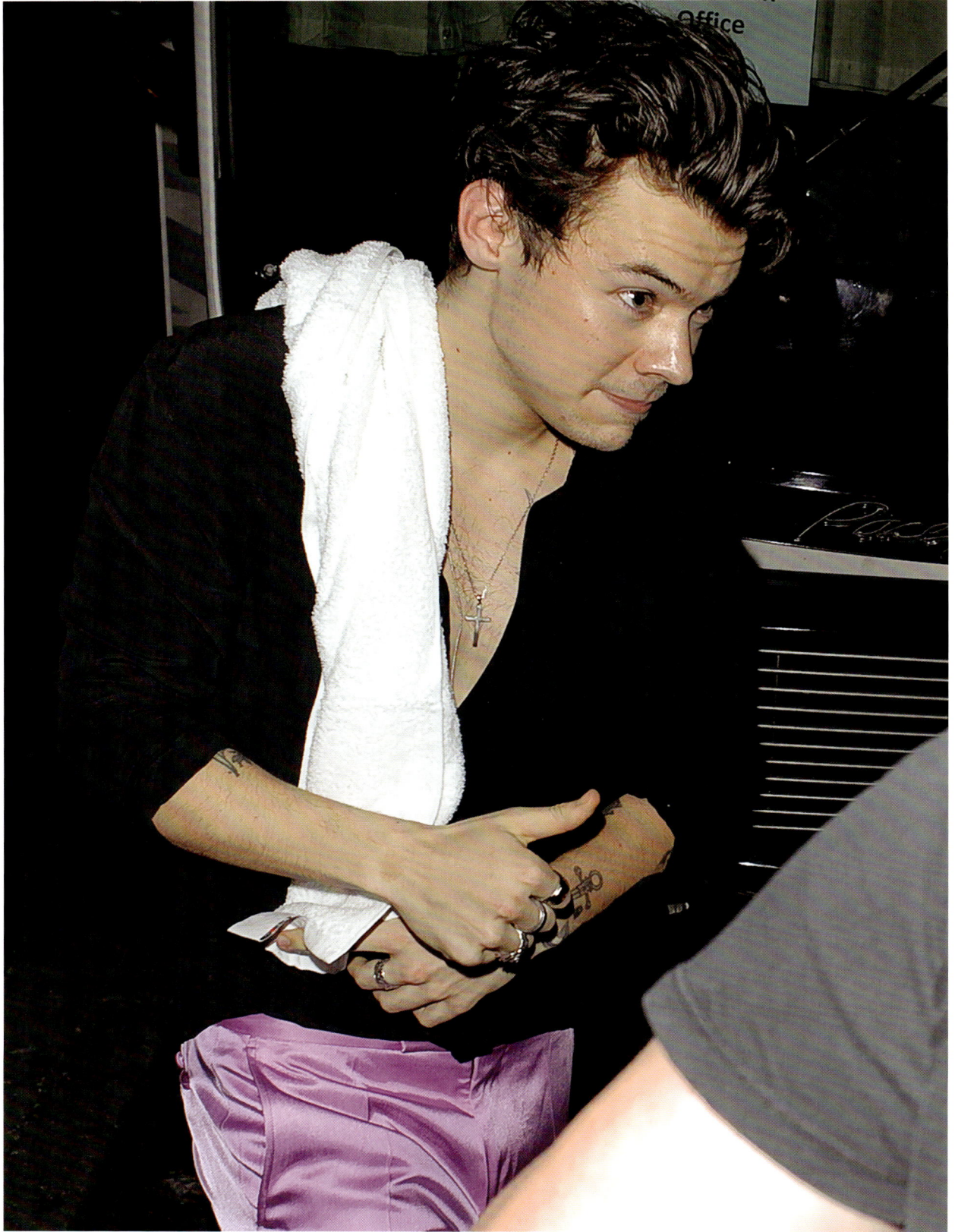

"To have time to live with a song, see what you love as a fan, chip at it, hone it and go for that ... it's heaven."

HARRY STYLES

"A lot of my influences, and the stuff that I love, is older," he told *Rolling Stone*. "I didn't want to put out my first album and be like, 'He's tried to re-create the '60s, '70s, '80s, '90s.' Loads of amazing music was written then, but I'm not saying I wish I lived back then. I wanted to do something that sounds like me. I just keep pushing forward." Styles also wanted to create an album he *enjoyed* hearing. "We just wanted to make what we wanted to listen to, and that has been the most fun part for me about making the whole album," he told Nick Grimshaw on the BBC *Radio 1 Breakfast Show*. "In the least weird way possible, it's my favorite album to listen to at the moment."

By late March 2017, Styles was ready to pull back the curtain and show the world what he had been working on, in the form of an enigmatic teaser video. As haunting piano music plays in the background, he walks through clouds of smoke toward a door that's slightly ajar. Harry then fully opens the door, letting a beam of light shine through so he's seen in silhouette. After a brief close-up of his eyes, a date flashes on the screen: April 7.

That ended up being the premiere day of his debut solo single, "Sign Of The Times." Calling it "the song I'm most proud of writing" on the BBC's *Radio 1 Breakfast Show*, he compared the release experience to a lengthy gestation: "I feel like I've been hibernating for so long ... and now it's time to give birth." To no one's surprise, the song went straight into the UK singles charts at No. 1 and spent seven weeks overall in the Official Charts Top Ten. In the US, "Sign Of The Times" debuted at No. 4 on the *Billboard* Hot 100. Styles was on his way to solo stardom.

A month later came the song's music video. It was a stunning and cinematic clip: Styles, clad in a long navy-blue coat, wanders around the Isle of Skye in Scotland, looking a bit lost. At one point, however, he steps off a rock and suddenly rises into the air as if an unseen force lifts him upwards. This kicks off a panoramic trip that finds Harry flying over picturesque forests, gorgeous waterfalls and a body of water with a rippling whirlpool, before ending the journey by ascending into puffy clouds and a brilliant sunset. According to *Billboard*, the video's stunt pilot claimed the musician reached a height of more than 1,550 feet while filming—and "no green screen or CGI effects" were used for the stunning scenes. Unsurprisingly, the clip ended up winning British Artist Video of the Year at the 2018 Brit Awards and received two MTV Video Music Awards nominations.

Previous Page: Harry Styles: Live On Tour, Madison Square Garden, June 21, 2018, in New York City

Opposite: Leaving a secret gig at the Garage in Islington, May 13, 2017, London, UK

The video and single release set the stage for the May release of *Harry Styles*, which was also an immediate hit. Buoyed by several high-profile promotional appearances—for a performance in New York City's Rockefeller Plaza, fans slept outside overnight for days to get the best viewing spot—the album topped the charts in multiple countries around the world, including Australia, the US, UK, Ireland, and Canada, and helped Styles start to gain a toehold as a solo artist.

The day after *Harry Styles* hit stores, he announced a last-minute show at London venue The Garage—his first-ever official solo concert. Sporting the crisp pink suit he favored during this era, Styles greeted the crowd politely—"Hello, London. I'm Harry; nice to meet you"—and ran through a set of songs from *Harry Styles*. However, he also covered Kanye West's "Ultralight Beam" and strapped on a guitar to perform One Direction's "Stockholm Syndrome."

Styles's friend Stevie Nicks (who he had met following a Fleetwood Mac concert in 2015) told *Vogue* that she was proud he achieved so much on his own terms. "Harry could've lost a lot of fans, but he didn't. I'm so proud of him because he took a risk and didn't go the One Direction route. He loves One Direction, I love One Direction, and a gazillion other people do too, but Harry didn't wanna go the pop route. He wanted straight-up rock and roll circa 1975." Fittingly, for Harry's debut American solo show at iconic Los Angeles club the Troubadour, Nicks was on hand to provide moral support and musical good vibes. She also performed three songs with him, including a cover of her Don Henley duet "Leather and Lace."

When Styles launched a global tour—titled, simply, Harry Styles: Live on Tour—he continued to put a dividing line between One Direction and his solo work. Although he added a few more older songs to his setlist (including, at various times, the One Direction tunes "If I Could Fly," "Story Of My Life" and "What Makes You Beautiful") he also performed a tune he wrote for Ariana Grande ("Just A Little Bit Of Your Heart") and cover songs; for example, a stripped-down version of Little Big Town's "Girl Crush" and a barn-burning take on Fleetwood Mac's "The Chain."

On special occasions, Styles also performed a few very unique songs. At a June 2018 concert at Madison Square Garden, Kacey Musgraves joined him onstage for a languid cover of Shania Twain's "You're Still The One." Strumming an acoustic guitar, he belted out the second verse in a tender voice, and harmonized perfectly with Musgraves on the chorus. Meanwhile in Australia he sang snippets of Rickie Lee

"He loves One Direction, I love One Direction, and a gazillion other people do too, but Harry didn't wanna go the pop route. He wanted straight-up rock and roll circa 1975." STEVIE NICKS

Jones's "The Horses," a nod to the fact that the Australian icon Daryl Braithwaite had a massive hit with his version of the song in 1991.

On this tour, Styles also debuted the non-album-track "Medicine," which immediately became a fan favorite. Musically, the song's galloping grooves and jagged electric guitar riffs echo seventies glam rock. Thematically, "Medicine" also nods to glam's fluid sexuality; the song's lyrics reference hooking up with a guy and winkingly describe sex as having the restorative power of medicine.

Styles initially wrote the song for his debut album, but it didn't make the final cut. Years later, he told Howard Stern he enjoyed performing "Medicine" live and wasn't sure why he discarded it—and explained why the tune *still* hadn't been included on his solo albums.

"I really love the song," Styles reassured. "I think I get kind of in my head about if there's a song that didn't make an album before, I'm kind of like 'Well, if it didn't make that one why would it make this one?' It feels older to me and I just feel better about the stuff that we're making in terms of what we're gonna put out now."

That relentless push forward—coupled with a remarkable ability to avoid being overly sentimental about the past—is indicative of Harry's solo career. But it's also one reason why he became so successful, so fast. He's always honored his past music and achievements—but has never let them overshadow whatever he's doing in the future.

Right: Performing live onstage during Harry Styles: Live On Tour, Madison Square Garden, June 21, 2018 in New York City

FASHION ICON

Harry Styles didn't become a cutting-edge fashion icon overnight. Just ask his mom, Anne Twist, who took at least partial credit for the pop icon's love of sartorial experimentation. "I was always a big fan of doing fancy dress with [Harry and his sister Gemma] when they were smaller, which Gemma hated but Harry always embraced," she said in a 2020 interview. "But you know, who doesn't love playing dress-up?"

As an adult, Styles certainly never passes up an opportunity to rock an eye-catching outfit—or do fancy dress. His looks might include bright patterned jumpsuits cut to show off his tattoos, tailored pants with a decided seventies flair or even a dress or kilt. "What women wear. What men wear. For me it's not a question of that," Styles told *The Guardian* in 2019. "If I see a nice shirt and get told, 'But it's for ladies.' I think: 'Okaaaay? Doesn't make me want to wear it less though.' I think the moment you feel more comfortable with yourself, it all becomes a lot easier."

Although a close relationship with Gucci means he's often sporting suits from that brand, Styles is also not afraid to mix and match interesting pieces or colors. At the 2020 Brit Awards, he paired a bright yellow Marc Jacobs suit with a lilac blouse, while past looks have included the following: a Gucci brown mohair suit with an applique dragon iconography; a purple iridescent Alexander McQueen suit; and a sweater vest with a sheep pattern. Accessories-wise, Styles is known for statement necklaces—ones with pearls or chunky beads—as well as multi-hued nail polish, retro sunglasses, and colorful feather boas.

Styles embarked on this bold fashion journey while still with One Direction. He drew raves for his updates of classic looks—for example, a black Saint Laurent suit with Chelsea boots—and more specifically his 2015 American Music Awards outfit: a white Gucci suit with detailed black flowers over a black dress shirt. "It was very exciting to see everyone's responses, but also how great he looked in it," stylist Harry Lambert told *Vogue*. "At the time it was a very bold move to make."

The suit set a precedent, as it wouldn't be the last time Harry's outfits turned heads. Many of these striking looks came courtesy of Lambert. The "Two Harries" crossed paths in 2014 and have worked together since on some of Styles's most memorable outfits. "Look, when it comes to this [gender stuff], I wish I could be all: 'I wanted to change the world!'" Lambert told *The Guardian*. "But it's more that it's a byproduct of what we're doing."

If anything, he sees his work as part of a long continuum of innovative pop music fashion. "If you look at pop icons over the years, fashion is such an integral part of their image, like Björk in the swan dress, Britney in the schoolgirl outfit," Lambert adds. "I'm aware that what I do is having an impact, but is that top of the agenda for me? No."

Styles has also found a kindred soul in Alessandro Michele, Gucci's former creative director. Speaking to *Vogue*, he revealed he admires Michele for being "fearless with his work and his imagination. It's really inspiring to be around someone who works like that." As an example, Styles appeared in *At the Post Office*, a 2020 short film included as part of a series called the *Ouverture of something that never ended* that was co-directed by Michele and Oscar winner Gus Van Sant. In

Left: At the 2023 Annual Grammy Awards wearing a custom, rainbow-colored patterned jumpsuit by Egonlab in collaboration with Swarovski

Opposite: With One Direction at the American Music Awards in 2015. Harry's bold Gucci suit turns heads and marks the start of his fashion journey.

the clip, he rocked cutoff jorts, loafers, high white socks, and a pink Gucci-branded T-shirt.

"Harry is now a friend," Michele told *Vogue* in 2020. "He has the aura of an English rock-and-roll star—like a young Greek god with the attitude of James Dean and a little bit of Mick Jagger—but no one is sweeter. He is the image of a new era, of the way that a man can look."

Styles showed off this new era especially while modeling for a 2018 Gucci Tailoring campaign. The photo shoot was very much in line with his character, as it found him hanging around a low-key North London fish-and-chip shop wearing smart, modern suits. Perhaps the most memorable photo finds him wearing a dark turquoise jacket with a maroon collar and pale pink embroidered flowers. He's looking like he's about to order some food—and he's inexplicably (but amusingly) holding a chicken in his arms.

Harry's fashion confidence grew as his musical career took off. As a co-host of the 2019 Met Gala—alongside fellow music icon Lady Gaga, tennis superstar Serena Williams, *Vogue* editor Anna Wintour, and Alessandro Michele—Styles wore a black sheer blouse with frilly accents, high-waisted black pants, low-heeled black dress boots, and pearl earrings. In a sign of his commitment to the outfit, he even pierced his ears specifically for the occasion.

Lambert told *Vogue* that Harry's Met Gala look was "elegant" and "camp, but still Harry," as well as being a departure from his onstage attire. "This look is about taking traditionally feminine elements like the frills, heeled boots, sheer fabric and the pearl earring, but then rephrasing them as masculine pieces set against the high-waisted tailored trousers and his tattoos."

For the Met Gala after-party, Styles deliberately channeled another notable pop era: the early 1980s New Romantic movement popularized by bands such as Duran Duran and Spandau Ballet. He paired the high-waisted black pants with a puffy white blouse and gigantic red bow, as well as a large cross earring in his right ear.

Styles made even bigger headlines in 2020 when he became the first man ever to appear by himself on the cover of *Vogue*. His outfit of choice was a ruffled light blue Gucci dress with black accents and a black blazer.

Previous Page: (L–R): Serena Williams, Harry Styles, Alessandro Michele, Lady Gaga, and Anna Wintour at the 2019 Met Gala

Left: The famous Gucci jacket and dress worn by Harry Styles for his 2020 Vogue cover

> ## "If I see a nice shirt and get told, 'But it's for ladies.' I think: 'Okaaaay? Doesn't make me want to wear it less though.'" HARRY STYLES

"Clothes are there to have fun with and experiment with and play with," Styles said in the accompanying cover story. "What's really exciting is that all of these lines are just kind of crumbling away. When you take away 'There's clothes for men and there's clothes for women,' once you remove any barriers, obviously you open up the arena in which you can play."

The choice of outfits provoked discussion and debate, with the magazine *Dazed* publishing an article, "Just how revolutionary is Harry Styles's *Vogue* cover?" that explored the ins and outs of the fashion decision. Still, Styles was undeterred and continued embracing unexpected fashion choices. A winter 2021 *Dazed* magazine cover feature led to photos involving a who's-who of fashion brands: Prada, Balenciaga, John Galliano, Burberry, Comme Des Garçons Homme Plus, Jean Paul Gaultier Archive.

As a result, Harry's looks were playful and unexpected, conjuring things like whimsical *Alice in Wonderland* figures; the bewitching vibe of Stevie Nicks; and Shakespearean characters. Outfits included a moss-green skirt and oversized sweater with polka-dot tights; a bright red wool sweater and matching shorts with the same tights; a frilly, black floor-length duster with a pink-and-black polka-dot underlay; and a cream-colored outfit comprising a cotton corset, mohair distressed sweater, and cotton and jersey shorts, along with white tights and black leather kitten-heel shoes.

Outside of fashion spreads, Styles continued to be adventurous. At the 2021 Grammy Awards, Harry followed up his green feather boa and black leather Gucci suit combo with another colorful outfit from the fashion brand: a lavender feather boa over a plaid yellow suit coat, a striped sweater and chocolate-brown corduroy pants. That the outfit resembled one worn by Cher Horowitz—the fashionable main character in the 1995 movie *Clueless*—caught the eye of Alicia Silverstone, who portrayed the iconic Cher. "I am loving the *Clueless* vibes, Harry Styles!!" Silverstone tweeted. "Cher would be so honored (and totally approve!!) of this chic look."

At the 2023 Brit Awards, Styles walked the red carpet wearing custom Nina Ricci by Harris Reed, in the form of a black tailored suit and a gigantic black satin organza oversized flower cushioning his neck. And at the 2023 Grammy Awards, he paraded a custom, rainbow-colored patterned jumpsuit produced by Egonlab in collaboration with Swarovski.

Incredibly, the latter suit featured 250,000 multicolored crystals and took more than 150 hours to create. "This unique custom-made piece is a transcription of Harry's aura and his fearless approach to fashion," a rep for Egonlab said in a press release. "The powerful color combination is a visual metaphor for his personality, his commitment to self-expression and total acceptance."

Despite so much evidence to the contrary, Styles told *Dazed* in 2021 that he doesn't consider himself a style icon. What matters more to him is "bringing people together," as he put it. "[At my shows] I get kind of a front-row seat to see a bunch of people getting in a room together and just being themselves. Not coming to the front of the stage, because they're hanging out at the back, dancing like nobody's watching." A few sentences later, he summarized this power to a tee: "A room full of people just loving each other is so powerful."

HARRY STYLES

RELEASED: MAY 12, 2017

A bold, confident solo collection indebted to warm 1970s pop-rock that established Styles as a contemporary pop icon

Expectations were sky-high for Harry Styles when he announced his debut solo single, "Sign of the Times," in March 2017. Not only was he moving on from one of the biggest pop groups ever, One Direction, but he had also been working on music for well over a year by that point. Outside of his inner circle, nobody was quite sure what Styles would look *or* sound like as a solo artist.

Any lingering anxieties quickly dissipated once "Sign of the Times," the lead track from his self-titled debut, hit the airwaves. A panoramic ballad blooming with languid beauty—think a gorgeous hot-air balloon inflating to its full glory—the single combines solemn piano, scorched guitar twang, measured drums, and a gospel choir. Styles alternates between an anguished falsetto and his usual keening midrange, shedding most vestiges of his glossy pop background.

Thematically, the song's lyrics suited the sonic grandeur. Styles told *Rolling Stone* that "Sign of the Times" is quite a serious tune, "written from a point of view as if a mother was giving birth to a child and there's a complication. The mother is told, 'The child is fine, but you're not going to make it.' The mother has five minutes to tell the child, 'Go forth and conquer.'" Fittingly, the song ends with a piano that sounds like an angel ascending to heaven. This was heady, serious stuff, and reviewers took notice, comparing "Sign of the Times" to luminaries such as David Bowie, Pink Floyd, and Elton John.

As it turns out, "Sign of the Times" was something of an outlier on *Harry Styles*. Working mainly with a core group of songwriters and musicians—Jeff Bhasker and his colleagues Tyler Johnson and Alex Salibian, engineer Ryan Nasci, and guitarist-drummer Mitch Rowland—Styles crafted a taut collection of warm, classic-sounding pop-rock. "Two Ghosts" resembles cozy singer-songwriter fare; "Meet Me in the Hallway" is shimmering psychedelic pop; "Sweet Creature" leans into golden-brown acoustic folk; and "Only Angel" explodes like a swaggering Rolling Stones rocker. Other additional instruments contribute pleasing variety: Viola and violin snake through several tracks, while Styles himself also contributes Omnichord in a few spots.

In other words, *Harry Styles* contains the kind of earnest hits that populated the Top Forty in the 1970s—a bold update of One Direction's music, which itself took cues from various shades of 1970s rock. However, Styles and his collaborators also very deliberately made sure the album wasn't too retro-sounding; in fact, multiple songs take a fresh spin on contemporary music. "Ever Since New York" possesses echoes of Beck's moodiest music, between the cascading harmonies and lush instrumentation; "Kiwi" bears a passing resemblance to The White Stripes; and "Woman" is diffracted funk that's somewhere between Elton John and Tame Impala.

This modern edge was important, as Styles was determined that the album reflected who he was—and what he had gone through in real life. This was especially true lyrically. "I didn't want to write 'stories,'" he told *Rolling Stone*. "I wanted to write my stories, things that happened to me. The number-one thing was I wanted to be honest. I hadn't done that before." In some cases, Styles was jaw-droppingly frank. For example, "Carolina" is based on a real life encounter, Styles told the BBC. "I wrote this and it felt like the bit of fun it [the album] was missing. It's about a specific person, and they know it's about them now." (Given that Styles names the person in the lyrics, it's a poorly kept secret.) "Kiwi," meanwhile, is about a vibrant, wild woman who's irresistible despite being rather over-the-top.

Elsewhere, many songs on *Harry Styles* address painful miscommunication or even breakups. "Meet Me in the Hallway" is about the agony of a crumbling relationship; "Sweet Creature" addresses a tempestuous relationship; "Two Ghosts," which Styles originally wrote for One Direction's last album, describes a couple who have lost their magic and now seem like invisible strangers to each other; and "From the Dining Table" oozes with regret over a partnership that's fading away without closure.

In the end, *Harry Styles* was a blockbuster smash around the world, landing at No. 1 in the US, UK, Ireland, Mexico, and countless other countries. Styles also made it abundantly clear that he was ready to make the transition from boy band member to solo artist—and had the confidence needed to forge an entirely new path for himself without missing a beat.

CHAPTER 5:

LIGHTS UP

Artists often find their second album difficult to write, especially if their debut was successful. Chalk that up to expectations: Once people know what they're capable of, there's pressure to produce more great work that equals (or surpasses) the quality of their first album.

Harry Styles found himself facing this kind of dilemma as he approached writing what would become his second album, *Fine Line*. With the 2017 release of his self-titled debut, Styles successfully distinguished himself as a solo artist outside of One Direction. The album topped the charts around the globe and enabled Styles to embark on a well-received worldwide tour. Momentum *and* goodwill were on his side.

However, Harry felt a bit stressed as *Fine Line* started coming together. "I felt like it had to be big," he told NPR. "The last record wasn't really a radio record: The single ['Sign of the Times'] from it was a six-minute piano ballad, so it wasn't the typical formula. So I felt a bit of pressure that I wanted to make something that worked." Complicating matters further, Styles added that feeling pressured actually *didn't* help him write the songs he wanted. "That's when I make the music that I like the least, is when I'm trying to write a pop song or I'm trying to write something fun."

As with his debut, Styles took his time finding his way forward for *Fine Line*—and relied on his collaborators for support. He reunited with Tyler Johnson and Kid Harpoon, both of whom had also appeared on *Harry Styles*, and let their collaborations unfold organically. They didn't book a series of regimented recording sessions in order to churn out a whole batch of potential songs. Instead, *Fine Line* was "made with a bunch of friends getting into the studio to see what happens," Kid Harpoon told *Music Week*. As it turns out, this collaborative chemistry made getting into a creative groove easier. "A lot of the best songs that came out weren't by anyone in particular," he added. "Harry was driving the vision, but the input came from everyone."

A great example of this is "Cherry," which Styles said emerged in the wee hours of the morning. He was hanging out with Johnson and collaborator Sammy Witte, drinking tequila and waxing philosophical about the future. "I was saying how I have all these records that I'd love to make, I love all this kind of music and in five years I want to make *this* kind of record, and in 10 years I want to make *this* kind of album, and then I'll get to make the music that I really want to make," Styles told NPR. "And Tyler just said 'You just have to make the music that you want to make—right now. That's the only way of doing it, otherwise you're going to regret it.'"

Left: Harry Styles greets a large crowd of fans outside BBC Broadcasting House, December 2019

That reality check woke Styles right up—and the crew ended up tracking "Cherry" that very night. Other songs came together just as spontaneously. Kid Harpoon revealed that "Falling" emerged from an impromptu recording session: He had dropped by Harry's house to give him a ride somewhere, and as he waited for the musician to get ready after a shower, he noodled around on the piano. Styles started singing along and "Falling" was done an hour later; he didn't even stop to get dressed, he confessed to *Rolling Stone*: "I was completely naked when I wrote that song."

Both of these songs happen to be about the aftermath of his low-key romantic relationship with the model Camille Rowe. (That's even her speaking French at the start and end of "Cherry," a slightly petulant song that obviously comes from a place of deep hurt.) Styles and Rowe dated for roughly a year from mid-2017 through summer 2018, and by all accounts their breakup affected Styles while making *Fine Line*. "It's not like I've ever sat and done an interview and said, 'So I was in a relationship, and this is what happened,'" he told *Rolling Stone*. "Because, for me, music is where I let that cross over. It's the only place, strangely, where it feels right to let that cross over."

In a nod to Styles's penchant for self-reflection and growing musical sophistication, these lyrics are thoughtful and even unsparing. For example, on "Falling," he holds the mirror up to himself and his actions—there's a reference to him acting out of line due to drinking—and isn't quite sure he likes what he sees in the reflection. "The chorus says, like, 'What am I now? Am I someone I don't want around?'" he told Apple Music's Zane Lowe. "It was a big moment where I was kind of asking myself, 'What am I doing?' I kind of started to feel threads of where I could see myself becoming someone that I didn't want to be."

Still, *Fine Line* is far from a brooding breakup record. The breezy "Watermelon Sugar" coalesced during what Kid Harpoon called a "catch up" in a Nashville recording studio while Styles was on tour. Much later, Styles revealed the song's meaning from the stage of a show, mischievously noting it's about "the sweetness of life" before adding, "It's also about the female orgasm, but that's totally different. It's not really relevant."

This open-minded attitude also had something to do with where Styles recorded. Among other places, he decamped to Malibu, California's Shangri-La studio, a place owned by the producer Rick Rubin. That studio was conducive to loosening up—Styles described things like frozen margaritas at ten in the morning and chocolate edibles chilling in a fridge—and expanding your mind. "We'd do mushrooms, lie down on the grass, and listen to Paul McCartney's *Ram* in the sunshine," he told *Rolling Stone*. "We'd just turn the speakers into the yard."

Such an idyllic atmosphere helped Styles get in the proper headspace to make a different record, one that sounded ebullient and lighter despite its sometimes-weighty source material. As Styles put it to Zane Lowe, he felt "so much more joyous" this time around. "And I was with my friends and we were in Malibu ... I felt so safe. It was like, 'I want to take some mushrooms? I'm going to take some—like now is the time to have fun.'"

Styles used several grand gestures to announce this new era. In early October 2019, mysterious posters popped up around the world featuring the phrase "Do You Know Who You Are?" in big white letters on a black background. Several days later, on a date that happened to coincide with World Mental Health Day, Styles also unveiled a website called *Do You Know Who You Are?* After visitors typed in their name, they would receive pep-talk compliments from Styles like "You are one of a kind" and "You are remarkable."

As it turns out, this promotion heralded the release of *Fine Line*'s first single, "Lights Up." (In fact, the phrase was actually a line from the tune.) A marked evolution from the sound of Styles's debut album, the song boasts a chilled-out R&B groove with stuttering beats; a chorus with Bowie-circa-*Aladdin Sane* piano and a twisting, minor-key melody; and a bridge with gospel-tinged vocal catharsis. In an interview with Capital FM, Styles described the song as being about "freedom and, I guess, self-reflection, self-discovery," he said. "I guess a couple things that I'd kind of thought about and, I guess, wrestled with a little bit of the last couple of years and then, I think, the song's kind of about me just accepting those things."

The music video for "Lights Up" embodied those ideas. Throughout the clip, Styles is shirtless and glistening with sweat while dancing and writhing with a group of people spanning all genders, ostensibly at a party. At other points in the video, he rides on the back of a scooter, his arms out like he's flying; looks at himself in the mirror as if he's peering at a stranger; and is shown both standing and floating in a body of water. The imagery and moody lighting within these scenes calls to mind heaven, hell

Above: Harry Styles, December 2019, onstage at The O2 in London

and purgatory—a canny commentary on worrying about the consequences of your actions—but also seems to depict Styles going through a baptismal rebirth or coming into the light; both are a figurative way of looking at self-discovery.

Many fans noticed that the "Lights Up" video premiere happened to arrive on National Coming Out Day, and wondered if that was Styles himself coming out or at least subtly sending a message about his sexuality. This chatter was nothing new: Since the start of his career, Styles has been asked about his sexuality—and asked to define his sexuality, sometimes rather directly.

In a 2015 GQ interview, the journalist asked him, "So you're not bisexual?" to which Styles responded: "Bisexual? Me? I don't think so. I'm pretty sure I'm not." Upon the

"I was with my friends and we were in Malibu ... I felt so safe. It was like, 'I want to take some mushrooms?...like now is the time to have fun.'" HARRY STYLES

release of his debut album, a journalist for *The Sun* brought up sexuality in pop music. "Everyone should just be who they want to be," Styles replied. "It's tough to justify somebody having to answer to someone else about stuff like that." The interviewer then asked if Styles had "personally labeled his sexuality" to which he replied he hadn't ("I've never felt the need to really") and affirmed, "I don't feel like it's something I've ever felt like I have to explain about myself."

Indeed, Styles has been a long-time vocal ally for the queer community. For example, starting with his initial solo tours, he took to waving various colorful flags (such as the rainbow pride flag or blue, pink, and white trans flag) during shows as a sign of solidarity. During the *Fine Line* era, the conversation around Harry's sexuality coincidentally started buzzing again thanks to the album's striking cover art, which happened to use the bisexual pride colors (pink, purple, and blue) and featured Styles sporting a magenta blouse.

The palette and his outfit didn't escape the notice of fans—although some people wondered about the optics of an ostensibly cisgender straight man using LGBTQ-associated imagery. Styles addressed the question honestly in a 2019 profile in *The Guardian*. "Am I sprinkling in nuggets of sexual ambiguity to try and be more interesting? No," he said, while adding, "In terms of how I wanna dress, and what the album sleeve's gonna be, I tend to make decisions in terms of collaborators I want to work with. I want things to look a certain way. Not because it makes me look gay, or it makes me look straight, or it makes me look bisexual, but because I think it looks cool." For good measure, he then once again affirmed his stance on where he stood on definition. "And more than that, I dunno, I just think sexuality's something that's fun. Honestly? I can't say I've given it any more thought than that."

In a 2022 *Better Homes & Gardens* interview, he used the term "outdated" to describe demands to define sexuality into a neat box. "I've been really open with it with my friends, but that's my personal experience; it's mine," he said. "The whole point of where we should be heading, which is toward accepting everybody and being more open, is that it doesn't matter, and it's about not having to label everything, not having to clarify what boxes you're checking."

This dislike of labels certainly extends to the trend-defying music Styles was making circa *Fine Line*. However, by not being concerned about how his music was perceived—or how *he* was perceived—Harry opened himself up to even more success.

"Lights Up" reached No. 17 on the *Billboard* Hot 100 but peaked at No. 3 in the UK, setting the stage for even greater things to come.

"I'm just trying to go through life being a little less worried about stuff," Styles told Zane Lowe. "If you don't hit the top of the chart, your life doesn't change. If that was what I was aiming at, and then it didn't happen, then I'd feel so much worse. But redefining it for me has been amazing to be like, 'Oh, but that's not the game I'm playing.' There's a freedom with that."

Leading up to the release of *Fine Line*, Styles didn't embark on a tour right away, although he did support the album with multiple appearances and performances. One of these was on November 16, 2019, when Styles hosted and performed on *Saturday Night Live*; as part of this gig, he showcased live versions of "Lights Up" and "Watermelon Sugar." Harry had previously been a musical guest on *Saturday Night Live* with both One Direction in 2014 and as a solo artist shortly after the release of his eponymous debut album *Harry Styles*. Sporting a glittery plum suit and hot pink nail polish, Styles crooned "Lights Up" accompanied by a pianist, guitarist, three backing vocalists and, later, a trumpet player, sounding like a cross between a solemn hymn and torch song. "Watermelon Sugar" was more upbeat and funky, thanks to a full horn section and a breezy, tropical-getaway groove. Fittingly, Styles almost looked like the juicy fruit, as he rocked a suit with a red shirt and pinkish jacket and pants.

This appearance presaged another mysterious promotional push: travel-style advertisements for a quaint seaside town named Eroda, complete with a website (visiteroda.com) and picturesque photos. Fans soon figured out it had to do with Styles, thanks to Easter eggs on the website; for example, multiple phrases referenced song titles on *Fine Line*. The end result was a music video for a new single, "Adore You," with Scotland-filmed scenery standing in for the fictional village of Eroda.

The premise was adorable: Styles finds a golden fish in the ocean and takes it home to care for it. Bizarrely, however, the fish becomes very big, very fast—outgrowing a fishbowl, clear backpack and, eventually, even a gigantic aquarium tank. Along the way, he and Styles bond—the adoration hinted at in the song reflects their relationship—which leads to some silly moments; for example, at one point both Styles and his fishy friend are pictured busting out some dance moves to the laid-back grooves of "Adore You." In the end, however, it becomes clear that the kindest thing Styles can do for the fish is let it live in the ocean, where it will be able to swim unencumbered.

Above: Live onstage during the 2021 Grammy Awards

A week after the "Adore You" video premiered, *Fine Line* landed in stores. Styles celebrated the occasion with a special show in Los Angeles at The Forum and then another one at the Electric Ballroom in London. In early 2020, he continued making the promo rounds, including a memorable March appearance on *The Howard Stern Show* during which he and his band performed a smoking cover of Peter Gabriel's "Sledgehammer"; Styles in particular showed off a soulful vocal delivery that was quite Gabriel-esque.

Unfortunately, the COVID-19 pandemic, which presaged the UK lockdown in March 2020, halted some of Harry's *Fine Line* promotional plans; most notably, he had to postpone his intended tour dates. However, not even a lockdown could stop his commercial surge. In the UK, five singles from *Fine Line* reached the Top Forty. Over in America, "Adore You" was also a hit, peaking at No. 6, although Styles's biggest achievement was yet to come: During summer 2020, "Watermelon Sugar" became his

"I'm just trying to go through life being a little less worried about stuff. If you don't hit the top of the chart, your life doesn't change." HARRY STYLES

first *Billboard* Hot 100 No. 1 hit in America, reaching that peak for a week in August.

The "Watermelon Sugar" video was also delayed due to the pandemic, but its emergence was a breath of fresh air during a very fraught time. Taking place on a gorgeous beach, the video is full of hedonistic behavior and suggestive gestures, many involving eating various pieces of fruit. Visually, its colors and fashions are retro-cool, as if Styles and crew had stepped back in time.

Directors Bradley & Pablo (Bradley Bell and Pablo Jones-Soler) told *LBB Online* that Styles and creative director Molly Hawkins had a very specific vision in mind: "They wanted to basically dedicate this song to girls and boys and sexual pleasure; it was about creating an atmosphere." For reference, the duo handed the directors two old photos. One featured Jack Nicholson "eating a watermelon with this amazingly mischievous grin," Bradley & Pablo said, while the other featured Sir Paul McCartney attending a 1960s beach party "where he looks like he's tripping on acid in the best way."

At the 2021 Grammy Awards, Styles performed a dynamite new arrangement of "Watermelon Sugar," transforming it into a 1970s soul-funk seduction complete with a horn section and backing vocalists. The bridge of the song evolved even more, into a zoned-out psychedelic rock breakdown; in response, Styles did a groovy choreographed dance with the vocalists while a trumpeter unleashed a cosmic improvised solo. His outfit suited the vibe: He draped a sea-green feather boa over a custom black leather Gucci suit with no shirt underneath.

That same night, Harry won his first Grammy Award, taking home Best Pop Solo Performance for "Watermelon Sugar." Clearly nervous and maybe a little in awe of the honor, Styles made a very humble acceptance speech. "To everyone who made this record with me, thank you so much," he said up front, noting "Watermelon Sugar" was the first song written after the release of his debut album. Styles then thanked his co-writers Mitch Rowland, Tyler Johnson, and Kid Harpoon, as well as his label and manager, before ending by giving kudos to his peers. "I feel very grateful to be here," he concluded. "All of these songs [in the category] are fucking massive, so thank you so much. I feel very honored to be among all of you."

At the time, little did Styles know that this award was just the beginning of another major career surge, one that would lead to bigger hits, bigger tours and the kind of ubiquitous stardom achieved by only very few musicians. In the moment, he was just soaking up the admiration for *Fine Line*—and enjoying the sweet rewards of success.

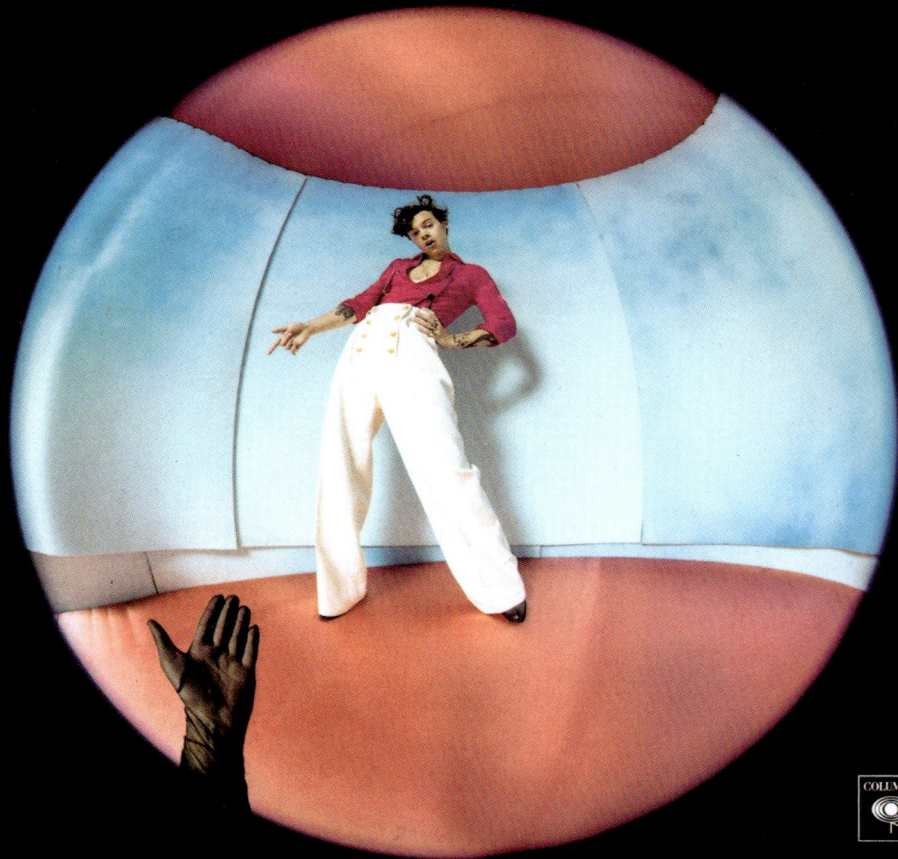

COLUMBIA

After releasing a successful debut album that challenged the boundaries of pop music, Harry Styles was ready to be even bolder as he approached his second solo effort, *Fine Line*. "I think I had a lot of fear, whether it was conscious or subconsciously, just about getting it wrong," Styles told NPR about his debut album. In hindsight, he can even tell how this affected the music. "I feel like I was almost bowling with the bumpers up a little bit. I can hear places where I was playing it safe."

Although *Fine Line* is once again influenced by the 1970s—including flowery psychedelic pop, David Bowie's proto-glam, campfire folk and soulful funk—the album certainly doesn't play it safe. The sprawling "She" is over six minutes long, with enigmatic lyrics, a zoned-out atmospheric vibe and some jagged-edge guitar work from Styles's musical collaborator Mitch Rowland. "Sunflower Vol. 6" resembles a cross between quirky eighties new wave and Tame Impala-esque electronic pop.

And though Harry describes "Canyon Moon" as "Crosby, Stills, and Nash on steroids," the shimmying folk song was inspired even more by another denizen of the Laurel Canyon scene: Joni Mitchell. In fact, Styles was so committed to channeling her on the song that he took a dulcimer lesson from Joellen Lapidus, the same woman who built the dulcimer Mitchell used on her 1971 album *Blue*.

Lyrically, *Fine Line* found Styles taking a cue from Mitchell and reflecting candidly on his life in the previous few years. While he gave *Rolling Stone* a pithy answer about the album's meaning ("It's all about having sex and feeling sad"), it's fair to say he experienced quite serious ups *and* downs—and extreme ones at that. "What I hadn't really experienced before during the making of this record, the times when I felt good and happy were the happiest I've ever felt in my life," he revealed to Zane Lowe. "And the times when I felt sad were the lowest that I've ever felt in my life."

"Golden" and "Adore You" talk about a relationship in happier times, while the title track addresses trying to find equilibrium within a tumultuous dalliance. Other songs are more explicitly about a broken relationship. His breakup with the model Camille Rowe informs "Cherry," a wounded and jealous song written from the perspective of someone who isn't thrilled their ex has moved on and is thriving; the lyrics even explicitly ask them not to call their new partner "baby," a meaningful nickname.

Collaborator Kid Harpoon told *Rolling Stone* that Styles "had a whole emotional journey about her, this whole relationship," but he tried to remain encouraging. "I kept saying, 'The best way of dealing with it is to put it in these songs you're writing.'" Styles agreed, telling Zane Lowe about "Cherry" specifically: "I wanted it to be true to how I was feeling then, in that moment. It was all part of being more open and not like, 'I don't care.' You get petty when something's not going the way that you want, and 'Cherry' is pathetic in a way."

However, Styles was just as honest about his own faults, particularly on "To Be So Lonely," which also touches on his relationship with Rowe. In a callback to "Cherry," he says he doesn't deserve to be called "baby" anymore—besides, it's too painful anyway—and admits he was stubborn and jealous. Styles also notes he's reached the acceptance stage of the breakup; after getting all of the self-flagellation and sulking out of his system, he's okay with the chapter closing on the relationship.

It's no coincidence that maturity and depth are two hallmarks of *Fine Line*. Styles had found the right balance of like-minded creative souls and collaborators and was more confident about his songwriting instincts, giving him the space he needed to flourish. As a result, *Fine Line* amplified both his innate pop sensibilities and spirit of adventure—and became another enormous hit, reaching No. 1 in the US, Australia, New Zealand, and multiple other countries and peaking at No. 2 in the UK.

STEVIE NICKS FRIENDSHIP

They say you should never meet your idols. Luckily, Harry Styles didn't listen to that advice and actually did seek out and later befriend a legend he had long admired: Stevie Nicks, who has found fame both with the band Fleetwood Mac and as a solo artist.

Styles first met Nicks backstage at a Fleetwood Mac show. As a token of his appreciation, he brought her a gift: delicious, personalized carrot cake. "Piped her name onto it," he told *Rolling Stone*. "She loved it. Glad she liked carrot cake." The sweet treat was the beginning of a beautiful friendship that's led to live collaborations and deep creative mentorship.

Styles grew up listening to Fleetwood Mac, so he later admitted that becoming pals with Nicks was somewhat mind-blowing. "It borders on an out-of-body experience," he told NPR about being in the icon's orbit. "Every time I'm with her, you want to be, obviously, present, right? I'm trying to enjoy being with her and soaking in. But I think at the same time, while you're in the room with her, I'm sitting there thinking about being 10-years-old and singing [Fleetwood Mac's 'Dreams']."

However, the respect is mutual. "Harry writes and sings his songs about real experiences that seemingly happened yesterday," Nicks told *Variety* in late 2020. "He taps into real life. He doesn't make up stories. He tells the truth, and that is what I do." In a sign of her deep respect, she's often shown up during pivotal moments in his career to add musical support.

A week after the release of his self-titled debut album, Styles played at iconic Los Angeles club the Troubadour. Nicks was on hand to make the concert extra special by collaborating with Styles on several songs, including his solo tune "Two Ghosts" as well as Fleetwood Mac's 1975 classic "Landslide" and Nicks's 1981 solo song "Leather and Lace." Originally a duet with the Eagles' Don Henley, the latter song showed off the chemistry between Nicks and Styles: The pair harmonized together on the bittersweet song, their voices intertwining like they had been duet partners for decades.

It was far from the last time the pair would perform together. For starters, Styles sang "The Chain" with Fleetwood Mac at a 2018 benefit show. Later, at Nicks's March 2019 Rock & Roll Hall of Fame induction as a solo artist—she had been inducted as a member of Fleetwood Mac in 1998—Styles did the honors with a speech and performance. Sporting a bright blue Gucci velvet suit, he strapped on a guitar and dueted with Nicks on her 1981 hit "Stop Draggin' My Heart Around," taking the vocal parts originated by the late Tom Petty. The gravity of this performance wasn't lost on him: Styles flashed the occasional smile at Nicks, but overall had a very serious look on his face as he harmonized carefully with her and also belted out crucial lead vocal melodies.

His speech inducting Nicks was often hilarious. "Somewhere around 2005, 2006, this woman became God, I think we can all agree on that," he quipped. "On

Opposite: Stevie Nicks, 1975

Halloween, 1 in 7 people dress as Stevie Nicks. She is both an adjective and a verb. To quote my father, 'That was rather Stevie Nicks,' and to quote my mother, 'I Stevie Nicks that shit so hard!'"

However, the speech was also earnest and heartfelt, reflecting the times they spent together and the wisdom she imparted. "If you're lucky enough to know her, she's always there for you," Styles said. "She knows what you need, advice, a little wisdom, a blouse, a shawl—she's got you covered. Her songs make you ache, feel on top of the world, make you want to dance, and usually all three at the same time. She's responsible for more running mascara—including my own—than all the bad dates in history combined."

Later in the year, Styles sang "Landslide" again with Nicks at the Forum in Los Angeles at the launch event for *Fine Line*. To say she liked this record was an understatement: In fact, before they went onstage, Nicks passed him a note that compared the LP to *Rumours*, Fleetwood Mac's legendary 1977 album. "We cried," she told *Variety*. "He sang those songs like he had sung them a thousand times. That's a great songwriter and a great performer."

Although the reception for Styles was of course delirious, the crowd response for Nicks when she strolled onstage was pandemonium. By now old pros singing together, the version of "Landslide" on this night was tender and moving; during the bridge the musicians even danced together and then clasped hands briefly. Styles, meanwhile, unleashed some different vocal harmonies—a sign of his growing confidence around Nicks and the strength of their friendship.

CHAPTER 6:

HARRY'S HOUSE

In 2020, Harry Styles was ready to launch a massive tour to promote his second album, *Fine Line*. Unfortunately, he was forced to scrap these plans after the COVID-19 pandemic reached a climax in March, when a lockdown was announced for the UK, following other countries, who were similarly affected. Styles certainly wasn't the only musician in this situation. However, he felt the pause far more acutely than most, as it was the first time in roughly a decade he had *really* taken a break. The experience was disorienting, as he put it in one interview: "Suddenly, the screaming stopped."

This kind of go-go-go attitude had been ingrained in Styles because of his days in One Direction. As he told *Better Homes & Gardens*, being in the group was "all about how do you keep it going—and how do you get it to grow?" That mindset made him almost afraid to stop, he added. "There were so many years where, for me, especially in the band and the first few years coming out of it, I'd just been terrified of it ending," he said, "because I didn't necessarily know who I was if I didn't do music."

Given the fact that music venues were closed and in-person promotion was on pause, Styles had no choice but to figure out who he was outside of the spotlight.

Previous Page: Performing live onstage, May 2022, Coventry, UK

Right: Harry Styles live in New York City, at the Music Hall of Williamsburg, February 28, 2020

And so while it was a leap of faith, he ended up chilling out from making music as the pandemic began. Harry moved into a house with three friends and did normal things such as preparing dinner and taking walks. "Suddenly you're forced to not be this musician guy," he told Zane Lowe. "You're forced to be a friend and a brother and a son. And I actually feel like I had a little bit of a chance to focus on that at least for a moment."

As it turned out, his artistic pause didn't last long. Styles eventually captured that emotional whirlwind with studio sessions *outside* of his house. He and his long-time producers/co-writers, Kid Harpoon and Tyler Johnson, had decided to live together and see what kind of musical magic might emerge from being in such close proximity. In a stroke of luck, Rick Rubin's Shangri-La Studios, where Styles recorded *Fine Line*, also happened to be available, and so the trio moved in.

"We didn't really know what we were going in for," he told *Rolling Stone*. "It just felt like sitting at home doing nothing might feel better if we all move in together and try to make some music." The first song he and Kid Harpoon wrote together for *Harry's House*—on the first day they were in the studio, no less—was "Late Night Talking," a light-touch soul-funk number with smooth grooves and a sizzling chorus hook.

Opposite: Live onstage at the iHeartRadio Secret Session, the Bowery Ballroom, New York City, February 29, 2020

"Suddenly you're forced to not be this musician guy. You're forced to be a friend and a brother and a son. And I actually feel like I had a little bit of a chance to focus on that at least for a moment." HARRY STYLES

It was an encouraging sign—and a song that Styles saw as a guidepost of sorts for the rest of *Harry's House*. "It set the tone for the intent with which, like, the album was made," he told BBC Radio 1. "When we wrote this one, we felt like it was really good, and then it kind of let us, like, relax a little bit ... like okay, if there's nothing else, we feel like we did some work."

In a wide-ranging interview with Zane Lowe, Harry outlined how the concept for *Harry's House* continued to evolve from these initial days. Originally, he viewed the collection as something "very kind of literal and on the nose"; more specifically, he thought about recording a cozy acoustic EP at home. (Accordingly, Styles named *Harry's House* in homage to *Hosono House*, the 1973 solo LP by the influential Japanese musician Haruomi Hosono, known for his work with the electronic music pioneers Yellow Magic Orchestra, and several bands—including the psychedelic-leaning group Apryl Fool and folk rockers Happy End.) However, having this unscheduled stretch of time put Styles in a meditative mood and he started to question his motivations for creation. "[I] looked at what I turn to listen to and what I was watching and all that kind of stuff," he said, "and was like, 'What does it actually mean to make something? And what does it mean to me to make something as my job?'"

Once Styles started digging more into making *Harry's House*, he had additional philosophical insights about the idea of home—and realized it was also less literal than he first thought. "[Home] wasn't about geographical location," Harry said. "It was much more of an internal thing ... [and] it felt like it took on this whole new meaning." More specifically, he pictured it more like a chronicle of his eclectic daily existence. "Imagine it's a day in my house; what do I go through?" he said. "A day in my mind; what do I go through? In my house I'm playing fun music, sad music, I'm playing this, I'm playing that. It's a day in the life."

Above: Pictured with his late stepdad, Robin Twist in 2014

Opposite: Haruomi Hosono pictured in 2019. His 1973 album Hosono House *influenced Styles during the making of* Harry's House.

To ensure the creative juices kept flowing, Styles and his band tried not to put too much pressure on themselves. Instead, they listened to their instincts and worked when they felt inspired. "We used to book a studio and be like, 'Okay, we've got it for two months, grind it out,'" Styles told Lowe. "But some days you just don't want to be there, and eventually you've been in the studio so long, the only thing you can write about is nothing because you haven't done anything. So with this album, we'd work for a couple of weeks and then everyone would go off and live their lives."

That process led to "Cinema"—which Styles wrote both at home and in the studio—and provoked fruitful bursts of inspiration. "Daylight" for example, came together in a marathon all-night session that ended with Styles and his band at the beach watching the sunrise. "We were like, 'We have to find a way to stay awake and finish this, because if we all go to bed, then this won't turn out the way it would if we finished tonight,'" he said.

The sessions for *Harry's House* eventually went global. In addition to recording at Shangri-La, Styles and his band also hunkered down at Peter Gabriel's Real World Studios in Bath, England. For good measure, he also drew inspiration from travels around Italy and France—countries he was able to visit once pandemic restrictions loosened—and time spent back at home in London.

The trip to Italy was especially profound. Styles spent a leisurely few weeks there by himself decompressing and not worrying about keeping a schedule. "I felt much

more present than I'd been in a really long time," he told Lowe. "I'd walk around and I'd get a coffee and sit down and drink it instead of just being like, 'Oh, I'll get it and I'll walk with it, because I'm going somewhere.' I just relaxed a lot."

Harry then drove from Italy back to England by himself in a car owned by his late stepdad, Robin Twist, who had sadly passed away in 2017. On his trip, he listened to audiobooks, but also to some of Robin's jazz CDs that were still in the car. This experience was emotional, as it reminded him of the importance of family and made him think about things like having a better work-life balance. "I felt like I did a family thing," Styles said. "And I think maybe for 12 years, family things have not always [been] the priority in maybe the way that they should've been, or I would like them to be more of going forward."

Fans didn't know it at the time, but *Harry's House* was done when Styles finally launched Love On Tour in September 2021. He eventually revealed hints about the release, however. In March 2022, fans first discovered social media accounts (for example, a Twitter—now X—account called @youarehome) and a now defunct website (YouAreHome.co). The latter included a door that opened slightly to include random patterns—one follower noted these represented the covers of books Styles had been known to read—and then the album cover, which depicted him standing in a living room arranged upside down.

This aligned with the actual announcement of *Harry's House*, which came with a simple teaser video: Sporting a flowing white shirt and blue jeans—the same outfit he was wearing on the album cover—and a slight smile on his face that exuded mystery, he walked out onto a small stage as an outline of a house was lifted around him. *Harry's House* received a thumbs-up from none other than Harry's idol Joni Mitchell, who tweeted, "love the title"—coincidentally, she also has a song named "Harry's House"—in addition to Daryl Hall and John Oates, who responded with a house emoji.

A week later, Styles released *Harry's House*'s first single, "As It Was." Incredibly enough, it was the last tune he wrote for the album—composed in "my friend's front room in England's countryside," he told Hits Radio—and he initially wasn't sure if the song would make the final tracklist. In the end, however, it felt like a fitting song and sentiment to share. "It just felt like the thing I wanted to say, the thing I wanted to be doing and the kind of music I wanted to make coming back," he told the internet radio platform, Audacy.

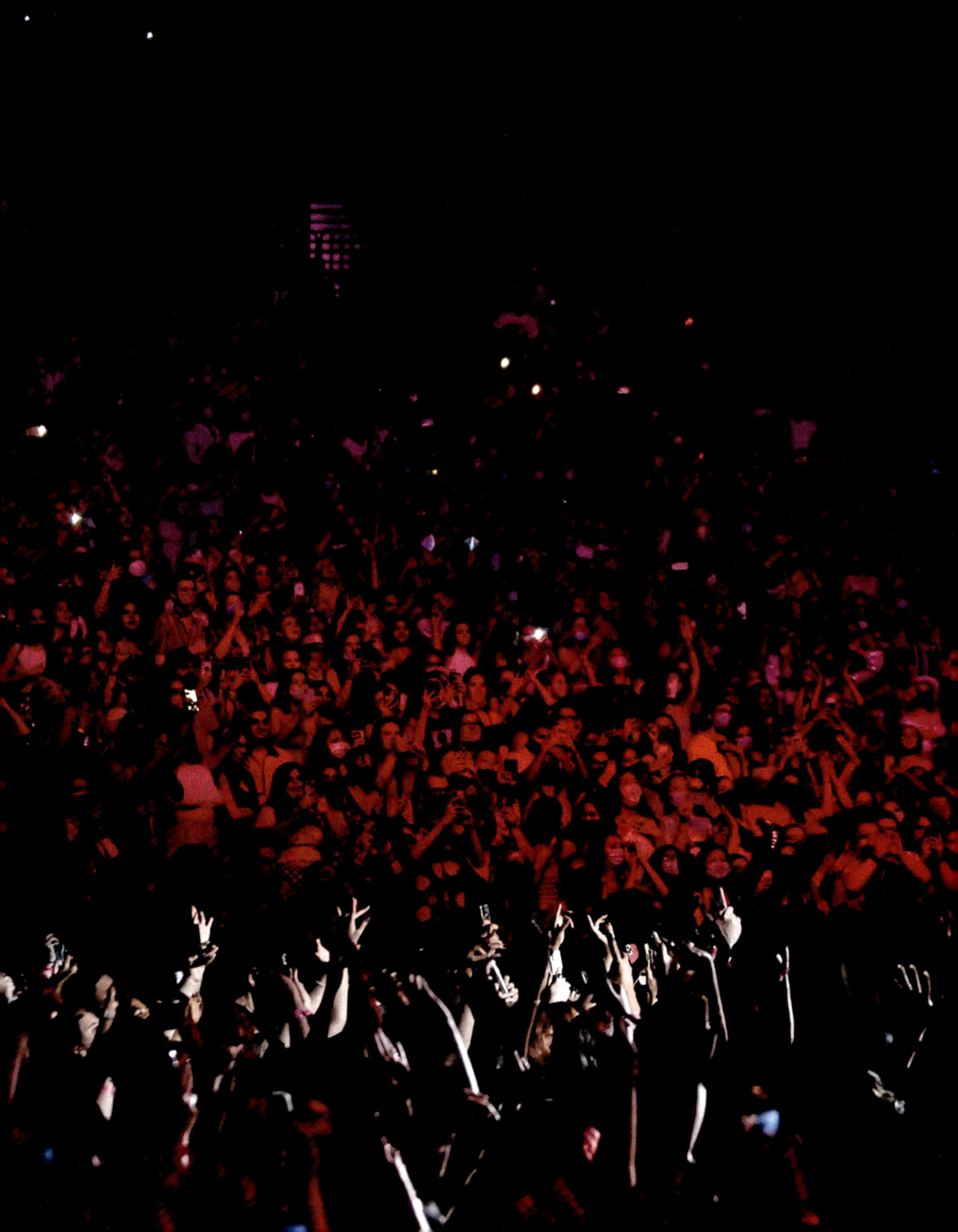

Previous Page: Harry Styles performs onstage during the tour opener for Love On Tour, MGM Grand Garden Arena, September 4, 2021, Las Vegas

Below: Performing live onstage on day 3 of BBC Radio 1's Big Weekend, May 29, 2022, Coventry, England

"... it's the first time I feel like I'm making music and putting music out from a real place of personal freedom." HARRY STYLES

"As It Was" starts with an adorable sample of Styles's five-year-old goddaughter, Ruby Winston, clamoring to tell the musician goodnight. Her voice is slightly pouty, a vibe explained by the fact that Styles apparently talked to her every night before she went to bed—but had skipped a call one night. ("She wanted to let me know that she was quite angry with me about it," he said in an interview.) From there, "As It Was" blooms into a short-and-sweet song driven by pitter-pattering rhythms, pogoing grooves and a bouncing-ball synth hook. It's certainly reminiscent of past songs—most notably, clever internet editors mashed up "As It Was" with a-Ha's new wave hit "Take On Me"—but the music also boasted refreshing buoyancy.

Thematically, "As It Was" also felt like something of a rebirth, albeit an ambiguous one. Speaking to NPR, Styles explained the song is "about metamorphosis and kind of losing yourself, finding yourself, embracing the fact that life hits you at different times, not when you expect it and, you know, change is scary." More specifically, the lyrics disclose that things in the world have changed—and although we're never explicitly told *why*, the narrator notes that the world is now simply "us." It's unclear whether that's a collective us or simply referring to people who have become a couple; Styles keeps things close to his chest even as he notes directly in one lyric that he's *not* better off alone.

However, it's also unclear whether all of these changes are *good*, because "As It Was" exudes more than a little hint of melancholy. But in the end, the song feels like a perfect encapsulation of the evolution Styles went through with the pandemic—and the changes he was still trying to reconcile.

The "As It Was" music video captured these complicated feelings. A marvel of cinematography, the clip was filmed at various places around London, including the Barbican Estate, which includes the Guildhall School of Music and Drama, and London Zoo's former penguin pool. The video first finds Styles walking forward and then backward within a hallway full of people thanks to some clever camera work. Then he takes off a coat to reveal a bright-red Arturo Obegero jumpsuit with diagonal iridescent stripes and does an intricate choreographed routine with dancer and model Mathilde Lin, who's wearing the same outfit in blue.

Standing and walking on a rotating platform that looks like a turntable, the couple embrace briefly—but in a nod to the song's references to disconnection, they often can't connect due to the circular movement. In another scene, Styles strips down to red swimming trunks and does another routine with Lin while on a floor full of bright

paintings. Finally, the video ends with Styles by himself, retracing his steps through all the places he's been and dancing in an ecstatic, unfettered way.

Appropriately, Styles told the SiriusXM *Morning Mash Up* he felt deep contentment upon the song's release. "I feel the most comfortable I've been with myself and happiest with what I'm making and the best I've felt about something that I'm making," he said, while adding, "I also feel really happy at the moment and I feel like it's the first time I feel like I'm making music and putting music out from a real place of personal freedom. And that is a really liberating place to [be] creating from and now putting it out."

Fans suspected there might have been another reason for this happiness, as they wondered whether several lyrics in the song (specifically ones mentioning two kids in context with a reference to not talk about the past) were veiled references to his current girlfriend, the actress and director Olivia Wilde. The pair—who co-starred in the 2022 film *Don't Worry Darling*, the movie that Wilde also directed and co-produced—were first spotted together holding hands at a January 2021 wedding. As the year unfolded, Wilde was spotted catching Styles gigs (and sporting a Love On Tour concert T-shirt) and the couple was also photographed together on vacation.

The duo were still going strong upon the release of "As It Was," despite heavy tabloid criticism about everything from their age difference (Wilde was a decade older than Styles) to her parenting skills; she shared two kids with her ex, the actor Jason Sudeikis. "When people see me not with my kids, it's always 'How dare she,'" Wilde told *Variety*. "I've never seen anyone say that about a guy. And if he is with his kid, he's a fucking hero."

Still, she and Styles decided to take the high road. "It's obviously really tempting to correct a false narrative," she told *Vogue*, in reference to the scrutiny of their relationship. "I think what you realize is that when you're really happy, it doesn't matter what strangers think about you. All that matters to you is what's real, and what you love, and who you love." Months later, Harry noted he also preferred to keep his personal life, well, personal—and used similar language Wilde used when talking about his long-standing policy of privacy. "I've never talked about my life away from work publicly and found that it's benefited me positively," he told *Rolling Stone*. "There's always going to be a version of a narrative, and I think I just decided I wasn't going to spend the time trying to correct it or redirect it in some way."

That confidence transferred over to "As It Was," which smashed streaming records and became Styles's second solo No. 1 hit in both the UK and US, spending

Opposite: Harry Styles and Olivia Wilde walk through Soho in London, March 15, 2022

(respectively) ten weeks and fifteen weeks atop the singles charts. For good measure, it topped the Canadian singles charts for an impressive eighteen weeks and also reached No. 1 in Australia, Germany, Ireland, Switzerland, and countless other countries.

Weeks later, on the day of *Harry's House* release, Styles performed a special concert at Long Island's UBS Arena. The streaming platform Apple TV broadcast the concert live, allowing fans to experience the show from anywhere. Styles ran through *Harry's House* and some other hits, to the great delight of fans. Prior to performing "Grapejuice," he even addressed the crowd, noting, "Your job is to have as much fun as you possibly can. If you want to sing, if you want to dance. Please feel free to do whatever it is you want to do."

Styles took this advice to heart, and even played "As It Was" twice. However, the show overall was an unqualified triumph. "We came offstage, and I went into my dressing room and just wanted to sit by myself for a minute," he told *Rolling Stone*. "After One Direction, I didn't expect to ever experience anything new. I kind of felt like, 'All right, I've seen how crazy it can get.' And I think there was something about it where I was ... not terrified, but I just needed a minute."

It's understandable he might feel a little overwhelmed: *Harry's House* topped the charts worldwide and earned 521,500 equivalent album units in the US during its first week on sale, the most successful week for any 2022 release until Taylor Swift's *Midnights* arrived months later. That same week, Harry also had four singles in the Top Ten of the *Billboard* Hot 100: the perennial hit "As It Was" as well as "Late Night Talking," "Music For A Sushi Restaurant" and "Matilda." With this feat, he became the first British solo artist *ever* to achieve such a milestone. The only other British act overall to land this many songs in the Top Ten? The Beatles.

Interestingly enough, Styles later admitted he considered naming the LP "Music For A Sushi Restaurant" after a visit to a Los Angeles sushi restaurant with his producer. "One of our songs came on from the last album, and I kind of said, like, 'This is really strange music for a sushi restaurant,'" Styles told NPR. "And then I was like, 'Oh, that would be a really fun album title.'" He eventually nixed the idea, but titled the album's opening track "Music For A Sushi Restaurant" instead.

This song also ended up having a memorable music video that resembled a mini-movie. In the science fiction-inspired clip, Styles portrays a half-human, half-squid creature who becomes the star attraction of a restaurant/club called Gill's Sushi. Despite his fabulous good looks and magnetic quality, Styles is treated like, well, just

Right: Kid Harpoon embraces Harry Styles after he wins Album of the Year for Harry's House *at the 2023 Grammy Awards*

another piece of fish. (Use your imagination as to what that might mean.) Much more lighthearted was the clip for "Late Night Talking," in which Harry's bed is a portal to other beds in all kinds of different places: a cheeky sleepover, an art gallery exhibit, a staid theater, and even a mobile bed that travels the streets of London.

Styles and Wilde made news headlines again in November when it was announced the couple was "taking a break," as *People* reported. "He's still touring and is now going abroad. She is focusing on her kids and her work in L.A.," a source told the publication. "It's a very amicable decision." Still, he looked for the silver lining. In mid-December 2022, Styles took to Instagram and posted a black-and-white photo of himself wearing a tracksuit and standing onstage before a show. "2022 changed my life," he wrote as a caption. "I can't begin to thank all of you who supported me through it, I'll never forget it. I hope your end of year is filled with happiness and calm. Love you all."

Things would only get better in 2023, as Styles's hard work paid off when the 65th Annual Grammy Awards rolled around. "As It Was" received four nominations— including in two of the biggest categories, Record of the Year and Song of the Year— while *Harry's House* was up for Album of the Year. At the February ceremony, Styles performed "As It Was" with a stage design that featured a spinning platform similar to the one in the song's music video. Although Styles looked great—courtesy of a silver Gucci suit with whirling fringe and sequins—things didn't go entirely as planned on the performance side.

As it turned out, the platform malfunctioned and put a huge wrench in the carefully planned choreography. "The moment the curtain opened, and it was time to perform, our turntable started spinning in reverse—backward," performer Brandon Mathis explained in a TikTok video. "Freaking all of us out on live television, and there was nothing we could do to stop it. So after a week of rehearsing this piece perfectly going this way, the moment it's time to perform it starts going this way." Impressively, Mathis added that the performers "had to troubleshoot and try to do a complete piece in reverse" on the fly, on live television—and while certain moments did seem off, the overall performance came over fine.

Luckily, Styles had a much better night on the awards front. *Harry's House* won Grammy Awards for Best Pop Vocal Album and Best Engineered Album, Non-Classical. It also took home one of the major honors: Album of the Year, triumphing over full-lengths by ABBA, Adele, Bad Bunny, and Beyoncé. Styles was the first British male solo

artist to win this category since George Michael, who won the award for 1987's *Faith*.

Styles was awarded his Grammy by a self-proclaimed superfan, a seventy-eight-year-old Canadian grandmother named Reina Lafantaisie. "I was so worried about messing up and reading the wrong name, but as I announced he had won, the room erupted in cheers," she said later. Styles also made sure that Lafantaisie was okay, however, as he bounded up the stage stairs and gave her a gigantic, lingering hug and kiss on the cheek while collecting his award. It wasn't their only interaction of the night: He also greeted Lafantaisie after winning Best Pop Vocal Album and sought her out when she was standing in a bathroom line, to acknowledge a card she left for him. "To my shock, he made a beeline for me," Lafantaisie said. "I couldn't believe how humble he was as he thanked me for, in his words, my beautiful card."

Lafantaisie ended up at the Grammys after becoming an internet darling thanks to a viral TikTok video from her granddaughter. In the clip, she passionately defends Styles and talks about why he's such a superstar; in the process, she coined a viral catchphrase: "Don't keep correcting me, I'm talking about Harry Styles!" In a later interview, she elaborated on why she was such a Styles fan. "I listen to his music all day long, as his songs put me in such a great mood and his lyrics say everything you need to know about him," Lafantaisie explained. "He oozes love and kindness and is such an overall good person who radiates loving energy—our world needs more people like Harry Styles."

At the Grammys, hecklers marred the sweet moment of Harry's big win somewhat by trying to interrupt him and protest his win because they thought other

"He oozes love and kindness and is such an overall good person who radiates loving energy—our world needs more people like Harry Styles."

REINA LAFANTAISIE

Opposite: Taylor Russell. Harry Styles began a relationship with the actress in 2023.

artists deserved the honor more. Some attendees in the audience came to his defense, however: Taylor Swift—who was also spotted grooving to the performance of "As It Was"—and H.E.R. noticeably stood respectfully while Styles accepted his Grammy.

If Harry was rattled, he didn't show it, as his acceptance speech was typically humble. "I've been so, so inspired by every artist in this category with me at a lot of different times in my life," he said. "I think on nights like tonight it's obviously so important for us to remember that there is no such thing as 'best' in music ... This doesn't happen to people like me very often and this is so, so nice."

In May 2023, Styles ended up releasing the fourth and final single from *Harry's House*, "Satellite." A sleek synth-pop song, it came with an adorable video written and directed by Aube Perrie, who also helmed the clip for "Music For A Sushi Restaurant." This music video was much tamer, as it stars a little vacuum cleaner robot named Stomper who catches a glimpse of the Mars rover Curiosity, who has spent a decade exploring the Red Planet all by itself. As Styles performs a show at the Forum in Los Angeles, Stomper makes a break for it and has adventures all over the US. Ultimately, it ends up stargazing with a friend—Styles—outside a NASA building just as its batteries run out of juice. "Honored to be an inspiration to robots everywhere, @Harry_Styles," the official Twitter (now X) account for Curiosity tweeted after the video premiered.

After Love On Tour ended in July 2023, Styles rightfully kept a low profile, save for times when the tabloids spotted him hanging with rumored girlfriend Taylor Russell or launching his new line of Pleasing fragrances in London. He did cause massive internet buzz in November by debuting what appeared to be a closely cropped buzzcut while attending a U2 concert at the Sphere in Las Vegas. The Instagram account for Pleasing confirmed the dramatic hairdo by posting a portrait shot of Styles.

It was certainly a markedly different look—but coming on the heels of a rather transformative few years for Styles, it felt very much in character. As he shared with Zane Lowe some time before when speaking about "As It Was" and its themes, "Everyone is changing, and I think there's no reason to not approach music that way, and kind of let it change and turn out differently than you started. You don't always get to realize something happens, and you kind of look at it and be, like, 'Wow,' and then you get to decide whether that is devastating or brilliant, and accept the fact that it's probably both."

ACTOR

Some musicians dabble in acting work, doing the occasional cameo or guest appearance in a movie or TV show in addition to filming music videos. Not Harry Styles. Yes, he's known for elaborate music videos—both with One Direction and as a solo artist—but he's also hosted late-night TV shows, acted in big-budget Hollywood movies, and even guested on an iconic Disney Channel show. (That would be *iCarly*, when he was still in One Direction.)

Styles set the bar high for himself: His first movie acting role was portraying a soldier named Alex in Christopher Nolan's 2017 World War II-era thriller-drama *Dunkirk*, alongside co-stars such as (among others) Kenneth Branagh, Mark Rylance, and Cillian Murphy. "It's hard to know what to expect walking into an environment like that—and it was amazing," Styles told *The Big Issue*. "The first surprising thing was the scale of the production. You walk on set the first day and get taken aback by everything."

Styles's character is "very un-glamorous," Nolan told the *Daily Mail*. "It's not a showboating role." And despite already being a music star, he earned the gig just like any other actor, Nolan added: "Harry sent in a tape, and we liked the tape. And he joined the workshop, and that was that. It was a really old-fashioned process—and Harry's features, ability and demeanor fitted right in." In fact, Nolan liked Styles for the role precisely because he has "an old-fashioned face ... the kind of face that makes you believe he could have been alive in that period."

Dunkirk was a massive success, grossing $527 million worldwide. Styles also drew praise from critics, with *USA Today* writing that he "offers a surprising amount of grit and pathos," while *Entertainment Weekly* noted he was "solid" and "seamlessly blend[ed] into the ensemble." And his performance set the stage for future film work, as the actress-director Olivia Wilde later told *Vogue* that Styles's performance "blew me away—the openness and commitment."

Several years later, Styles and Wilde would work together on 2022's dystopian drama-thriller *Don't Worry Darling*. Set in the postcard-perfect California of the 1950s, the film finds Styles portraying a buttoned-up businessman named Jack who is married to Alice (Florence Pugh)—a whip-smart housewife who unravels a terrible secret, at great cost to everyone involved. Wilde appeared in the movie, but also directed and co-produced it. "I had a wonderful experience being directed by Olivia," Styles told Howard Stern. "Acting is very uncomfortable at times. I think you have to trust a lot." He also added: "Being able to trust your director is a gift. That was very helpful, and it really meant for a really nice experience working on that movie."

Styles also wrote a song for *Don't Worry Darling* called "With You All the Time" that's credited to Alice and Jack, his and Pugh's characters in the movie. "I remember first playing it on the piano, and it had a sort of homemade nursery rhyme feel to it," he told *Variety*. "Applied to the different moments in the film, I think it takes on a couple of different lives—I hope." The sparse song finds Pugh whisper-singing some simple lyrics (and having her voice occasionally manipulated) over a skeletal piano part. It's as disorienting as the movie itself. "I wanted something that could be both sweet and creepy, entirely dependent on the context," Harry added.

Critics weren't as kind to Styles for *Don't Worry Darling* as they were for *Dunkirk*. *The Atlantic* even ran an article titled "What Is Harry Styles Doing in *Don't Worry Darling*?" with the sub-headline "The only thing more disappointing about this movie than the screenplay is the singer's acting." *Vogue* was kinder, noting that while Styles "struggles in the scenes that demand fiery anger" he "believably conveys aching and angst, just as he does in his music."

In 2022, Styles also co-starred in the film *My Policeman*, portraying a closeted policeman named Tom who strikes up a relationship with a man named Patrick (David Dawson) while marrying a woman (Emma Corrin). The film is set in 1950s England where, at the time, being gay was outlawed, which adds tension and nuance. "It's obviously pretty unfathomable now to think, 'Oh, you couldn't be gay. That was illegal,'" Styles told *Rolling Stone*. "I think everyone, including myself, has your own journey with figuring out sexuality and getting more comfortable with it."

Director Michael Grandage had previously told *Vanity Fair* he envisioned the film's sex scenes as "quite literally show[ing] something that was about 'lovemaking' in the broadest sense of the word," a sentiment Styles echoed to *Rolling Stone*. "There will be, I would imagine, some people who watch it who were very much alive during this time when it was illegal to be gay, and [Michael] wanted to show that it's tender and loving and sensitive."

Harry's overall performance is indeed also very sensitive and generous, as he captures the conflicts within his character with nuance and grace. Speaking to *Rolling Stone*, he said he viewed the movie as having more universal love themes. "It's not like 'This is a gay story

Above: Filming a scene for
Dunkirk *in the UK, July 2016*

Previous Page: A film still from Don't Worry Darling, *2022*

Left & Opposite: James Corden and Harry Styles shooting a music video for "Daylight" on The Late Late Show with James Corden

about these guys being gay.' It's about love and about wasted time to me." During the movie's November 2022 red carpet premiere, Styles elaborated more on what he meant, noting the film's story is about how "it's never too late to follow your heart and do what you want," and added, "It's never too late to follow your happiness and be brave in love."

The latter comment is very much in line with Harry's long-time vocal support for the LGBTQ community and the way he encourages people to embrace their true selves. However, his *Rolling Stone* comments drew criticism in an article for *The Guardian* in which the author, in part, noted that "downplaying the film's queerness in a way that smacks of a past era's panic" resembles "an age-old tactic to make gay subject matter more appealing to timid, potentially prejudiced majority audiences." Critics were also once again split on his acting performance, although a *Newsday* review recognized his skill, observing, "If anyone is still

wondering whether the pop star Harry Styles can act, *My Policeman* should put all doubts to rest."

These weren't the only high-profile film roles Styles took on. In the end credits of the 2021 film *Eternals*, Styles was introduced into the Marvel Cinematic Universe as Eros, brother of Thanos. The future of this character is still rather unclear; in fact, it's still a mystery whether we'll see Styles-as-Eros in a movie again soon. "He's excited. We're excited. We will see," Marvel Studios President Kevin Feige coyly told *Entertainment Tonight* in November 2023.

In addition to his film work, Styles has also amassed plenty of television experience. A week after releasing his debut single, "Sign of the Times," Styles was the musical guest on *Saturday Night Live*. He performed not just that song but another new tune, "Ever Since New York." He also stretched his acting chops in several skits, highlighted by an exaggerated (but hilarious) Mick Jagger impression in a sketch involving the game show

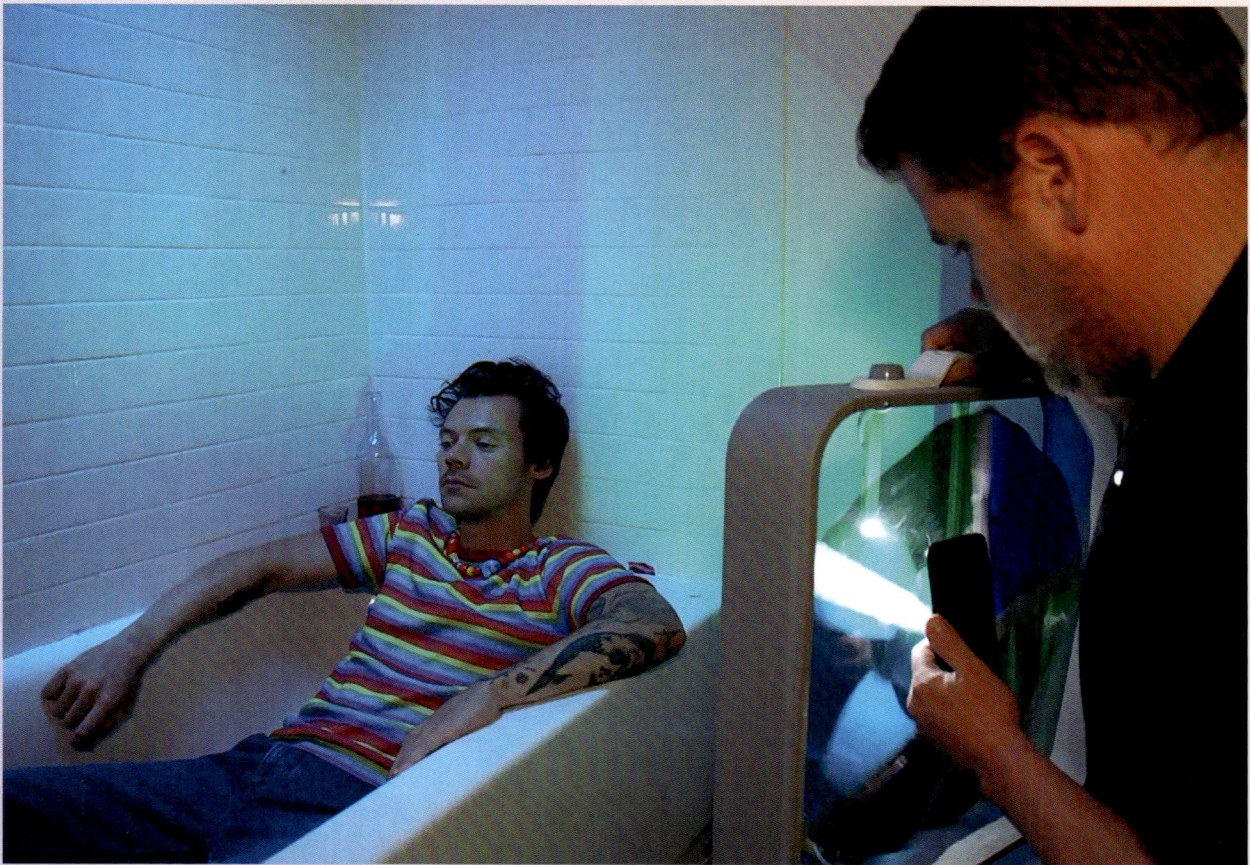

Family Feud. In November 2019, Styles earned his first *Saturday Night Live* hosting-performing gig and more than held his own doing comedy in sketches throughout the entire program.

Styles also had a close relationship with James Corden's late-night TV show, *The Late Late Show with James Corden*. In May 2017, he celebrated the release of his debut solo album with a week-long residency on the show. Not long after, he graduated to guest host—and did a dynamite job. In December 2017, Styles filled in doing the same role in *The Late Late Show* at the last minute, as Corden's wife was at the hospital having a baby girl. Two years later, he had even a bigger task while guest hosting the show: Not only did he deliver the nightly opening monologue, he interviewed Kendall Jenner—rumored to be a one-time flame of his—and also participated in a brief interlude of "Carpool Karaoke."

Furthermore, Corden encouraged Styles's musical endeavors. In May 2022, he and Styles teamed up to film a music video for *Harry's House*'s "Daylight" in three hours for just $300. The resulting behind-the-scenes chronicle of the filming is a delight, as the pair land on an apartment featuring a mega-Styles fan and her roommates, all of whom were game to put together a music video on a lark. The results are lo-fi and fun, centered on some special effects-laden rooftop scenes and a carefree apartment party.

With all this experience and success, it's fair to wonder whether Styles will concentrate even more on acting in the future. But as he told *Rolling Stone* in August 2022, it's a case of wait and see. "When you're making music, something's happening," he explained. "It feels really creative, and it feeds stuff. A large part of acting is the doing-nothing, waiting thing. Which if that's the worst part, then it's a pretty good job. But I don't find that section of it to be that fulfilling. I like doing it in the moment, but I don't think I'll do it a lot."

CHAPTER 7:

LOVE ON TOUR

I t's said that good things come to those who wait. That's certainly the case with Harry Styles's second world tour, Love on Tour, which was supposed to start in 2020, but ended up being postponed and rearranged due to the COVID-19 pandemic and instead kicked off in September 2021. The delay ended up being for the best: Harry's popularity skyrocketed in the meantime—among other things, he earned his first US No. 1 single with *Fine Line*'s "Watermelon Sugar"—and he had time to record an entirely new album, *Harry's House*.

Styles's concerts have long been known as welcoming safe spaces. As he himself told the audience at a November 2021 show in Detroit: "Please feel free to be whoever it is that you want to be in this room tonight." (He also expressed a similar sentiment at the rest of the tour dates.) But Love On Tour was particularly special: Coming after a very challenging few years for the world, the concerts became places that provided solace, community, much-needed connection, and escapist fun. Styles responded to these vibes with energetic performances full of ecstatic, unselfconscious dance moves, charming stage banter, and absolute gratitude for music.

The runaway popularity of Love On Tour allowed Styles to do some unique things, such as launch sold-out

Previous Page: Performing with Lizzo (L) at Coachella, April 22, 2022, in California

Left: Fans Arrive For Harry Styles: Love on Tour outside Madison Square Garden in New York City, August 21, 2022

Right: (L–R): Mitch Rowland, Sarah Jones, Jonathan Geyevu, Harry Styles, Pauli Lovejoy, Elin Sandberg, and Ny Oh on the set of The Howard Stern Show, *May 18, 2022*

residencies in various cities—including an eye-popping fifteen concerts at New York City's Madison Square Garden, twelve nights at the Forum in Los Angeles and six-show residencies in both Chicago and Austin. When the tour finally wrapped in July 2023 in Italy, Harry had sold five million tickets, for a total gross of $617.3 million, making it easily one of the highest-grossing tours ever.

Unsurprisingly, although Love On Tour started out in support of *Fine Line*, it ended up also being a tour to promote *Harry's House*. "By the time we went out touring, I'd finished [*Harry's House*] and I got to play those songs [from *Fine Line*] with the knowledge of what was next," Styles told Zane Lowe. "I feel like I got to hide a secret this whole time."

This wasn't always easy, he added, jokingly: "When I went into rehearsals for the tour, I had just been mixing the new album, so I had been listening to it constantly. And I guess in the first rehearsal, I'm trying to remember the words. What are these songs?" Setlist-wise, this meant that the shows received a big overhaul after the release of *Harry's House*, with many of his early songs jettisoned in favor of newer works. (Never fear, however: Styles made sure One Direction's "What Makes You Beautiful" *always* stayed in the setlist.)

Luckily, Harry's band could handle anything he threw at them. Although there were a few changes here and there as Love On Tour unfolded—among other things, Styles added a horn section, while keyboardist Niji Adeleye left after the 2021 dates and guitarist Madi Diaz hopped on for the 2023 UK and European legs—the core musical chemistry between the band members made all the difference.

"In the car with my mother as a child, this lady taught me to sing. She also told me that men are trash." HARRY STYLES

Percussionist Pauli Lovejoy brought the rhythmic bustle and good vibes—for example, high-stepping in unison with Styles during "Kiwi"—while bassist Elin Sandberg and keyboardists Yaffra and Ny Oh anchor the music with grooves and verve. Perhaps the most beloved member of the band, however, is badass drummer and vocalist Sarah Jones, whose energy and personality make her a fan favorite. The only musician that equals her popularity? Lead guitarist and vocalist Mitch Rowland, who happens to be married to Jones in real life.

Styles's outfits also evolved over the course of the tour. He started off generally wearing tailored pants and shirts in a rainbow of colors, but evolved his look to include things like feathered (or fringed) jackets, a series of jumpsuits in a heart pattern, or a vest-and-matching-pants set with tassels or shiny decals. During weekend one of his 2022 Coachella headlining gig, Styles sported a rainbow-sequin jumpsuit. He also brought out a very meaningful guest: country star Shania Twain.

As the opening chords of her late nineties hit "Man! I Feel Like a Woman!" rang out, she appeared at the top of the stage and strutted down the stairs to trade off dance moves with Styles. In turn, he belted out lines from the song with gusto—a testament to his formative years listening to Twain. "In the car with my mother as a child, this lady taught me to sing," Styles said after the first song, then drew laughs with the next line: "She also told me that men are trash." However, he then became serious, telling Twain: "To you, to the memories you gave me with my mother, I will be forever grateful. I'm so grateful you're with us here tonight." The pair then did a tender version of Twain's "You're Still the One."

During his weekend two set at Coachella, Styles brought out Lizzo—whose song "Juice" he had covered by himself *and* with Lizzo herself in early 2020—for a cover of Gloria Gaynor's "I Will Survive" and then One Direction's "What Makes You Beautiful." Wearing a gigantic fluffy pink coat and shiny magenta pants, he held his own especially on the former anthem, creating an empowering vibe.

Styles also debuted the *Harry's House* song "Boyfriends" at Coachella. "It's both acknowledging my own behavior [and] it's looking at behavior that I've witnessed," Harry told Zane Lowe. "I grew up with a sister, so it's watching her date people and watching friends date people, and people don't treat each other very nicely sometimes." The song dated from the *Fine Line* sessions, but he didn't want to push to include it on that album. In the end, Styles ended up doing "so many versions of it,"

Opposite: *Performing live onstage with Shania Twain at Coachella 2022*

he added, including one with vocals and acoustic guitar and another with electric guitar. On *Harry's House*, Ben Harper plays guitar on it, using the exact guitar he used to write his first three albums. "He'd gifted it to his daughter, and had to ask for it back to borrow to play it on the [song], but he didn't tell her what it was for, so I believe now will be her finding out where he played it," Styles revealed. "But thank you for letting us borrow it."

Coachella wasn't the only memorable Love On Tour show. For example, Styles celebrated Halloween in 2021 at Madison Square Garden with a two-night event dubbed a "Harryween Fancy Dress Party." He lived up to the theme, dressing like Dorothy from *The Wizard of Oz* on night one—complete with ruby slippers, rosy cheeks and a humble blue-checked dress—and a Pierrot clown (think David Bowie's "Ashes to Ashes" video) on night two. During the latter show, he also did a faithful, flirty cover of Britney Spears's "Toxic" that brought the house down.

At the 2022 Harryween in Los Angeles, he dressed like Danny Zuko from *Grease*, complete with a greaser hairdo and a black sleeveless shirt with the word "Harryween" in red glitter on the back. In honor of Olivia Newton-John, who played the role of Sandy in the film and had passed away in August 2022, he performed "Hopelessly Devoted to You" from the movie. Weeks later, he did another meaningful tribute to a musician who had passed on. In Santiago, Chile, he covered Fleetwood Mac's "Songbird" in honor of the lovely tune's writer, Christine McVie, who had just died. Gorgeous and understated, the performance very much came from Harry's heart.

When Love On Tour reached Australia in March 2023, Styles nodded to his 2018 visit to the country and

covered Rickie Lee Jones's "The Horses" in Melbourne and Perth. But then during his second concert at Accor Stadium in Sydney, Styles had a special guest to give him a hand with the cover: Daryl Braithwaite, the Australian legend who had a massive hit in 1991 with his take on the song. After bowing down and doing an "I'm not worthy!" gesture toward Braithwaite, Styles and his band did an appropriately faithful cover of "The Horses"; at one point, Braithwaite and Styles even harmonized in dreamy unity.

Beyond music, Love On Tour also featured some prominent show rituals. Dressing up was encouraged—and fans turned out with some amazing concert wear that carried on Styles's bold fashion sense—and elevated banter. Among other things, Styles oversaw baby gender reveals and marriage proposals and frequently joked with audience members. Song-wise, "Treat People with Kindness" especially turned into a venue-wide dance party. Conga lines snaked through the general admission floor sections of some venues, while others featured large groups of fans doing a well-choreographed line dance routine (aka the "boot scoot"). The scope and scale of the line dancing was incredibly impressive; in fact, Styles eventually took notice and even proudly did some adorable boot scooting of his own onstage.

Rituals at concerts are nothing new; in fact, they're a time-honored tradition that bond people together into permanent friendships, creating what can often feel like a shared secret language. When you're going through rough times or seeking out your path in life, the bonding aspect of fandom provides comfort and meaning. Moreover, this welcoming environment especially spoke to why Harry's music and presence resonated so much. Love On Tour was an oasis of acceptance.

"It's definitely feeling like there's a space where people feel safe enough to have those big moments and obviously share them with a room full of people and share them with us, in a way," Styles said of his concerts during a 2022 interview with Howard Stern. "[That's] probably one of the things I'm most proud of."

Ever humble, Styles deflects from taking credit for the "incredibly emotionally generous atmosphere" at his shows. "It's one of the first two things people comment on: 'I've just never been in an atmosphere like that,'" he continued. "It feels so safe. It's like a family full of strangers who are feeling this free evening. It's kind of an escape. I think the fans create that atmosphere more so than me."

When Stern pushed back and said Styles was the "lightning rod" and "catalyst" for all of this, the musician responded, "I wouldn't say I was a catalyst. I'd say I'm more of a

mirror. I only have that space onstage to feel free enough to be whoever I am because it's an environment that both the fans and people in my life, my friends, have created for me to feel like I can be whoever I want."

For years, Styles has worn or waved various flags given to him by fans during his shows—to name a few, the trans, pride, bisexual and lesbian flags. During Love On Tour concerts, he often used these flags to help fans "come out." For example, if someone wanted to announce they were bisexual or a lesbian, he might very dramatically raise the corresponding flag above his head, amping up the drama with some tension-filled music, and then proclaim that the fan had officially come out. It often felt like he was knighting someone or otherwise bestowing a massive honor on them.

(To be fair, Styles helping fans come out is nothing new: At a 2018 show, he read a sign held up by a fan named Grace that read, "I'm going to come out to my parents because of you." Upon learning that her mom's name was Tina—and she was at a nearby hotel—he then decided to "tell Tina before you have the chance to." A few moments later, he bellowed a phrase that immediately became part of Styles fan lore: "Tina, she's gay.")

These moments aren't just deeply moving—they're a sign of Styles's kinship and the deep care and respect he has for fans, as well as his desire to make his concerts an inclusive environment. Coming out is often a process that's fraught with anxiety or uncertainty—but Styles eases these feelings by ensuring someone has an entire arena (or stadium) cheering them on in positive, affirming support.

When asked about the various flags, he told *Rolling Stone* in 2019, "I want to make people feel comfortable

being whatever they want to be. Maybe at a show you can have a moment of knowing that you're not alone." Styles then acknowledged his privilege, adding, "I'm aware that as a white male, I don't go through the same things as a lot of the people that come to the shows. I can't claim that I know what it's like, because I don't. So I'm not trying to say, 'I understand what it's like.' I'm just trying to make people feel included and seen."

The latter desire also informed his public support for Black Lives Matter; for example, he affixed a sticker for the movement on his guitar and held up a Black Lives Matter flag during shows, including at a fall 2021 concert in Los Angeles. These gestures were significant, as Styles wasn't always so vocal about his stance. In fact, he drew criticism from fans after ignoring a Black Lives Matter flag thrown onstage during a 2017 London show.

But after the May 2020 death of George Floyd—who was murdered by a white police officer in Minneapolis—Styles became more outspoken, writing on social media, "Being not racist is not enough, we must be anti racist. Social change is enacted when a society mobilizes. I stand in solidarity with all of those protesting." With no fanfare, he also showed up at a Black Lives Matter march in Los Angeles and was pictured with friends.

"Talking about race can be really uncomfortable for everyone," Styles told *Variety* later in 2020. "I had a realization that my own comfort in the conversation has nothing to do with the problem—like that's not enough of a reason to not have a conversation." In other words, the introspection and self-reflection he had been doing during the pandemic that influenced *Harry's House* also extended to his non-musical life.

"I want to make people feel comfortable being whatever they want to be. Maybe at a show you can have a moment of knowing that you're not alone." HARRY STYLES

"Looking back, I don't think I've been outspoken enough in the past," Styles continued. "Using that feeling has pushed me forward to being open and ready to learn ... How can I ensure from my side that in 20 years, the right things are still being done and the right people are getting the right opportunities? That it's not a passing thing?"

That thoughtfulness most of all permeated Love On Tour. And it was clear Styles didn't want the tour to end. On July 22, 2023, the tour wrapped up at RCF Arena Campovolo in Reggio nell'Emilia, Italy. After the main set, Styles took to the piano and played a lengthy, untitled instrumental piece by himself that featured subtle horn and flute shading. It was somber and reflective—and hinted at an intriguing new sonic direction, if Styles wanted to go that route. But it was also achingly beautiful: The piece felt like he was giving Love On Tour a proper sendoff.

After the tour, he released a video, *Love On Tour, Forever*, that included clips of fans from all over the world interspersed with behind-the-scenes footage and performance clips. The video was beautiful, as it showed off the community that sprang up around Love On Tour—and demonstrated how diverse, beautiful and supportive Harry's fanbase is.

"We want to help each other and just be kind to each other and love each other," a fan said in the clip. "Those friendships are gonna stay after the tour and that doesn't end because the tour is ending. That's always going to be there." On Instagram, meanwhile, Styles shared additional thoughts about the tour. "It's been the greatest experience of my entire life. I feel so incredibly full and happy. It's all because of you. You have given me memories that will last a lifetime, more than I could have ever dreamed of. Thank you for your time, your energy, and your love."

After such a lengthy tour, it's understandable that Styles might not embark on another big trek again soon. But as the fan noted in the video, the impact of Love On Tour has endured even after the music stopped—and Styles for one couldn't be more thankful for the places his career has taken him. "Everything in my life has felt like a bonus since *X Factor*," Styles told *Rolling Stone*. "Get on TV and sing. I never expected and never thought that would happen."

TREAT PEOPLE WITH KINDNESS

When Harry Styles embarked on his first solo tour in 2017, he sold merchandise emblazoned with the phrase "Treat People With Kindness." The following year, he released a limited-edition T-shirt with this phrase in rainbow-colored text to celebrate Pride, with all proceeds going toward GLSEN, an organization that strives to provide safe and inclusive schools for LGBTQ youth. In 2018 he also sold hair ties with the slogan during Live On Tour, where profits went to local charities.

Incredibly enough, all of these things pre-dated the song "Treat People With Kindness," which ended up being on 2019's *Fine Line*. "I told Jeff [Bhasker], I would love to someday write a song called 'Treat People With Kindness,'" Styles told *Rolling Stone*. "And he was like, 'Why don't you just do it?' It made me uncomfortable at first, because I wasn't sure what it was—but then I wanted to lean into that. I feel like that song opened something that's been in my core."

Co-written by Bhasker and Ilsey Juber and featuring prominent lilting vocals from the duo Lucius and guitar from ex-Wings guitarist Laurence Juber, the upbeat song is relentlessly earnest, and features a skipping-on-the-playground groove and delicate strings. Unsurprisingly, "Treat People With Kindness" also boasts an underlying

Left: Lucius at the 2023 Grammy Awards

Opposite: *At the 2020 BRIT Awards, wearing a Treat People With Kindness badge*

Left: Ilsey Juber at the BMI Pop Awards, May 10, 2022, Beverly Hills, California

message that aligns with the title: It feels good to be in a place where you're being kind, and being in this state of mind can even be a comfort during tough times.

Styles also filmed one of his most memorable music videos for the song: Shot in black-and-white as if to mimic an old-fashioned musical, it features him dressed in a quite dapper outfit while leading a big band. This eventually evolves into multiple highly stylized dance sequences, including memorable ones in tandem with the actress Phoebe Waller-Bridge. The video is an absolute delight, as it illuminates the joy in the song and demonstrates the power of dance to foster connection —an idea fans would later pick up on during Love On Tour performances of the song.

After "Treat People With Kindness" was released, Styles continued to use the phrase on merchandise that benefits charities. In 2020, it appeared as part of a limited-edition shirt encouraging people to stay home and protect each other from COVID-19—proceeds went to the World Health Organization's Solidarity Response Fund—as well as socks that benefited a refugee charity called Choose Love.

However, "Treat People With Kindness" isn't just a song and a slogan. It's also an overarching ethos that informs his actions and fandom. Philanthropy is built into his concerts. By the end of Love On Tour, Styles had been able to donate $6.5 million to local charities around the globe, including Planned Parenthood, Physicians for Reproductive Health, Every Town for Gun Safety, Black Minds, and Black Voters Matter Fund – Capacity Building Institute. He also partnered with the nonprofit HeadCount to help 54,000 fans register to vote. This followed the impact of Styles's *first* round of

tour dates, Live On Tour, which raised $1.2 million for charity and also registered thousands of voters.

All of this builds on the causes Styles has supported over the years—a diverse list that includes being part of the #FirstSnog campaign for the LGBTQ rights charity Stonewall, sponsoring water wells in India via Drop4Drop, and donating his hair to Little Princess Trust, a charity that helps kids with hair loss obtain wigs. And this generosity is infectious: For example, fans celebrate Styles's birthday by coming together and raising money for charity. In 2019, that included more than $30,000 for LGBTQ organizations like The Albert Kennedy Trust, which helps LGBTQ+ sixteen to twenty-five-year olds who are unhoused or dealing with an unhealthy or dangerous living environment.

"I believe this is an opportunity for us to continue his message of kindness and ensure vulnerable youth can continue to have access to this wonderful charity's engagement," fan Sasha Wedge, who hails from Manchester, wrote on a personal fundraising page that generated more than $2,200. This was far from the only successful campaign overseen by Wedge: Previous years involved fundraising pushes for The Royal National Lifeboat Institution (RNLI) and Royal Manchester Children's Hospital.

At the end of the day, all of this kindness is wrapped up in gratitude, something Styles possesses in spades. "I hope you had as much fun as I did," Harry wrote on Instagram after the end of Love on Tour. "Look after each other, I'll see you again when the time is right. Treat People With Kindness. I love you more than you'll ever know."

HARRY'S HOUSE

RELEASED: MAY 20, 2022

"I realized that that home feeling isn't something that you get from a house; it's more of an internal thing."

HARRY STYLES

You can consider *Harry's House* to be Harry Styles's "pandemic record." After all, when he was forced to cancel long-awaited headlining tour dates, he hunkered down and secretly recorded the album in various studios in both the US and England. But instead of feeling claustrophobic or angry, the album is breezy and meditative—the sound of catharsis and introspection colliding in Styles's best solo album yet.

Among other things, the album reflects Harry's weekly commitment to therapy. "I felt like I exercise every day and take care of my body, so why wouldn't I do that with my mind?" he sensibly told *Rolling Stone*.

This led to insightful songs such as "Little Freak," in which he looks back at past failed relationships, as well as tunes such as "Cinema" and "Grapejuice" in which he muses about the nuances of new love. These moments are often delightfully detailed. "Keep Driving," for example, chronicles the intimate details of a relationship with playful language about a cozy breakfast: pancakes with syrup, coffee, hash browns and eggs. "Love of My Life" is about his love for England, even though it also scans like it's about a relationship. "I've always wanted to write a song about like home and loving England and all that kind of stuff," he told Zane Lowe. "And it's always kinda hard to do without being like, 'Went to the chippy and I did this thing.'"

Several other songs on *Harry's House* ruminate about the human condition. One of Styles's favorite songs on the album is "Matilda," which he named after the book character created by Roald Dahl. Styles told NPR he based the song on a real-life experience he had with someone, but wrote the lyrics as if he was having a conversation with the fictional character: "If you were

speaking to Matilda now that she's all grown up, who's been kind of mistreated by her family and stuff, how would you speak to her?"

Harry's House is a nod to *Hosono House* by Haruomi Hosono, a purveyor of the Japanese genre city pop, which takes influence from (among other things) late seventies and early eighties rock, funk, soft rock, and R&B. This sound is evident throughout *Harry's House* as multiple songs boast humid funk-R&B grooves: the mid-1980s homage "Cinema"; soft-glow soul-pop gem "Daydreaming"; and the horn-peppered "Music For A Sushi Restaurant." Other moments hew toward dreamier fare ("Little Freak") while "Love of My Life" and "Matilda" are deliberately stripped-back; the latter takes cues from indie-folk—and features cello from indie star Dev Hynes—while the former feels like a classic torch song. For good measure, John Mayer plays guitar on two songs, while Ben Harper contributes guitar to "Boyfriends."

Prior to making *Harry's House*, Styles also started listening to classical and instrumental music, including works by the jazz pianist and composer Bill Evans and composer Samuel Barber as well as the music of *Swan Lake*. Changing up his listening habits led to other influences. "You can reference things by the emotions they evoke," he told Zane Lowe, adding, "I wanted to step out of going like, 'I love that synth; let's find out what that synth is and get close to [it].'" Accordingly, *Harry's House* uses its instrumental palette for emotional impact, in large part by employing deliberate dynamics.

In the end, this thoughtful approach paid dividends with *Harry's House* winning a slew of awards, including Album of the Year at the MTV Video Music Awards and British Album of the Year at the Brit Awards, along with three Grammy Awards.

PLEASING

In a 2020 NPR interview, Styles noted that his fashion choices, like wearing nail polish, weren't meant to be a bold statement. "I do it when I'm not working, so to me it doesn't feel like it's 'Oh, I'm sending a message with my nail polish,'" he said. "I just put a lot less weight behind it, I think."

"And sometimes I forget, because I'll go somewhere and someone will be like 'Have you got nail polish on?'" he continues. "I'm lucky that I work in an industry that allows you to be creative and express yourself, and I'd encourage it to anybody."

Styles decided to help others express themselves with the make-up and lifestyle brand Pleasing which he launched in late 2021 with two partners: stylist Harry Lambert and his creative director Molly Hawkins. Pleasing's first offerings included four shades of nail polish, as well as primer serum and an eye and lip serum called the "Pleasing Pen."

In an interview with *Dazed*, Styles explained exactly why he wanted to branch out into make-up. For starters, it feeds his creativity—and aligns with what he's *already* doing. "It's starting with nail polish, because that was kind of the birth of what it was for," Styles said. "Me seeing a color on a flower or a wallpaper or something and thinking, 'Oh, I wanna put that on my nails.'"

However, he soon came to realize Pleasing represented "so much more than nail polish" and instead

Left: Harry Lambert, 2023

Above: The Pleasing Hot Holiday Caravan by Harry Styles at Dreamland Margate, UK, July 2022

also spoke to his emotional and sentimental sides. "I've always found that the moments in my life which have brought me the most joy are the small ones, whether it be, you know, the end of the night under the stars or a bite of food, or sitting with your friends thinking, 'Oh, I'm never gonna forget this,'" he said, adding, "I really think that the essence of Pleasing is finding those little moments of joy and showing them to people."

Accordingly, Pleasing prides itself on being eco-conscious—for example, "The Pleasing Pen" has ingredients like okra, marshmallow and lingonberry—while the nail polish is plant-based and 100 per cent biodegradable. The packaging is also as carefully curated as Styles's looks; for example, the glass nail polish bottles feature oversized sphere-sized caps and angular bottles.

"To succeed, the packaging needs to be interesting and exciting," Harry Lambert told *Fast Company*. "We want the products to be so gorgeous that they live on your shelf, not inside your drawer."

From an aesthetic perspective, Styles also wants Pleasing to be different from other companies and brands. "I think the true DNA of Pleasing is about working with talented people who might not necessarily have the light shone on them, and collaborating," he told *Dazed*. Accordingly, Pleasing works with up-and-coming artists and photographers—and also gives to charities such as Covenant House, Dress for Success and GlamourGals.

Since its initial 2021 splash, Pleasing has expanded into a full line of nail polish—with whimsical names

Harry Styles's love of nail polish gets The Pleasing range kickstarted: with a fresh manicure, February 14, 2020 (Left) and later at the BRIT Awards 2023 (Right).

Overleaf: Harry Styles, 2023

like Lion's Underpants (yellow) and Glorious Broken Heart (a shimmery blue-purple)—as well as hand and nail cream, a skin spritz, and pressed powder. They've also dabbled in apparel, with Styles memorably sporting "The Kissing Swan Knit," a brown sweater with two graceful white swans, in an Instagram ad in which he also debuted a close-cropped haircut.

And in the fall of 2023, Pleasing collaborated with the fragrance house Robertet for a trio of "distinct, genderless scents that embody simplicity, innovation, creativity, and beauty," with names like Rivulets and Closeness. There was some precedent: Styles had previously promoted Gucci's fragrance *Mémoire d'une Odeur*. Now that Pleasing is an established brand, it's become clear that the company is an extension of the thoughtful, inclusive career Styles is striving to build.

"I also think that what this can become is so much more than just products you can buy," he told *Dazed*. "I think it's about giving, and giving back. I am blessed to have fans who are so supportive of me, who believe in freedom and who have created this safe space for each other. Pleasing is really for them. That feeling of community is kind of what we would like Pleasing to [reflect]."

"I am blessed to have fans who are so supportive of me, who believe in freedom and who have created this safe space for each other. Pleasing is really for them." HARRY STYLES

"Everything in my life has felt like a bonus since *X Factor*. Get on TV and sing. I never expected and never thought that would happen." HARRY STYLES

SOURCES

Bibliography

Dare to dream: Life as One Direction. Harper Collins, 2011.

Magazines and Newspapers

The Atlantic, Better Homes & Gardens, The Big Issue, Billboard, Business Insider, Complex, Cosmopolitan, Coup de Main, Daily Mail, Dazed, Digital Spy, Fast Company, Gay Times, The Guardian, GQ, Hello, Hits Daily Double, Mirror, Music Business Worldwide, Music Week, NME, NPR, People, Pitchfork, Pop Sugar Rolling Stone, Seventeen, The Daily Record, The Hollywood Reporter, ScreenRant, The Standard, The Sun, The Sydney Morning Herald, USA Today, Variety, Voice of America, Vogue, Vulture, Warrington Guardian, Wired

TV and Radio

Apple Music, BBC, Capital FM, *Entertainment Tonight, Harry Styles: Behind the Album* (2017), Hits Radio, *The Howard Stern Show, The Late Late Show with James Corden,* MTV News, *Saturday Night Live,* SiriusXM, *The Today Show*

Websites

columbiarecords.com, justgiving.com, lbbonline.com, livejournal.com, narcity.com, needtoknow.co.uk, ninaricci.com, officialcharts.com, stylecaster.com, tumblr.com, worldradiohistory.com, (x) twitter.com, youtube.com

Picture Credits

ALAMY COVER, lev radin 10-11, 30-31, 40-41, 46-47, 52-53, PA Images 9, 60-61, Evan Agostini/Invision/AP 20 ARCHIVIO GBB 24, 49, 62-63, 154-155 WENN Rights Ltd 25 Vinyls 26 brinkstock 34-35 Doug Peters 44-45 Matt Crossick 50-51 UPI/John Angelillo 54-55, 70 Associated Press 64 Byron Purvis/AdMedia/Sipa USA 72-73 © Jason Moore/ZUMA Wire 74 © Twentieth Century Fox Film Corp. All rights reserved. /Courtesy Everett Collection 75 AP Photo/Mark Humphrey 78-79 Charles Sykes/Invision/AP 81 Amy Harris/Invision/AP 102 Imageplotter 106-107, 112-113 Scott Garfitt/EMPICS 110-111 Pjr news 136-137 Vianney Le Caer/Invision/AP 144-145, 146-147 AP Photo/Chris Pizzello 156-157 Moviestore Collection Ltd 187 JGY GETTY 2, 138-139 Anthony Pham 6-7, 189 Dave J Hogan 12, 166 Kevin Mazur/Getty Images for ABA 14 Steve Jennings/Getty Images for Sony Music 15, 148-149 Kevin Mazur/Getty Images for The Recording Academy 16-17 Jeff Spicer 56-57, 71 Al Pereira/WireImage 68-69 Jason Merritt/Getty Images for iHeartMedia 84-85 Terence Patrick/CBS 86-87 James Devaney/GC Images 88-89, 94-95, 160-161, 168-167, 170-171, 176-177, 179 Kevin Mazur/Getty Images for HS 90 GORC/GC Images 93 Kevin Mazur/Getty Images for Casamigos 97 Matt Winkelmeyer 98 Robyn BECK /AFP 99 Kurt Krieger/Corbis 100-101 Kevin Mazur/MG19/Getty Images for The Met Museum/Vogue 109 Dominique Charriau/WireImage 114-114 Rich Fury/Getty Images for Spotify 119, 120 Kevin Winter/Getty Images for The Recording Academy 125 Fin Costello/Redferns 126-127 Theo Wargo/Getty Images For The Rock and Roll Hall of Fame 128-129, 140-141 Joseph Okpako/WireImage 130-131, 174-175 Kevin Mazur/Getty Images for SiriusXM 132 Kevin Mazur/Getty Images for iHeartRadio 135 Jun Sato/WireImage 142, 188 Neil Mockford/GC Images 152 Karwai Tang/WireImage 158, 159 CBS via Getty Images 162-163 Alexi Rosenfeld 164-165 Cindy Ord/Getty Images for SiriusXM 173 Theo Wargo/Getty Images for HS 180 Michael Buckner/Variety 182 Leon Bennett SHUTTERSTOCK 18-19, 32-33 Mcpix Ltd 23, 181, 186 Richard Young 29, 36, 39, 42-43 Ken McKay 58 Startraks 66-67, 76-77, 134, 190-191 David Fisher 82 Broadimage 116-117 JM Enternational